CHRISTIAN TRAINI

LORD AND GIVER OF LIFE

An Introduction to the Person and Work of the Holy Spirit

Nigel Wright

Illustrated by June Gascoigne

Published by
The Baptist Union of Great Britain
December 1990

Designed, typeset and produced for the Baptist Union of Great Britain by
Gem Publishing Company, Brightwell, Wallingford, Oxfordshire.

Printed in Great Britain by Pike Printers, Kettering, Northamptonshire.

CONTENTS

Unit		Page
	Introduction	6
1	The Spirit – God on the Inside	11
	Assignment 1	
2	The Spirit and Creation	20
3	The Spirit and Revelation	26
	Assignment 2	
4	The Spirit as the Giver of Jesus	31
5	The Spirit as the Gift of Jesus	38
	Assignment 3	
6	The Spirit and the Church	44
7	The Spirit and the Believer	53
	Assignment 4	
8	The Spirit and the Future	66

PREFACE

This material on the Holy Spirit – *The Lord and Giver of Life* – has been prepared with several possible uses in mind.

CTP COURSE

It may be that you are planning to use this manual as part of the Christian Training Programme Diploma or Lay Pastor's Certificate Courses. If so, you will need to work your way through the units with the guidance and encouragement of your tutor and adviser, completing the assignments which are found at the end of Units 1, 3, 5 and 8. There are other suggestions for reflection and thought in the material which you will find of interest, but you will be assessed only on your response to those four assignments.

GROUP STUDY

You may have opportunity to use the material as the basis for study in a house group or some other study group. If this is the case, then you will find sections occurring frequently headed TO THINK ABOUT. These provide opportunities to stop and reflect on what you have been reading and especially to consider the practical application of issues which are raised. It is a proven fact that adults learn much in the mutual sharing of groups; so if it is possible to work through this material with others, you will be well rewarded.

PERSONAL INTEREST AND STUDY

There will be others who are neither working on a CTP course nor are part of a group, but who have an interest in this subject. There is much material here which will be helpful for private meditation and reflection.

Having completed your reading and study of this material, in whichever way you use it, you may feel you want to explore further some of the themes and issues raised. To help you do this, at the end of the manual is a list of books for study and reference.

Unless otherwise stated, Bible quotations are from the New International Version.

However you use this manual, our hope is that you will find it useful both in understanding more fully the Person and Work of the Holy Spirit and in experiencing more deeply his ministry in your Christian life and service.

Paul Mortimore
Editor

INTRODUCTION

The aim of this study manual is to expand our understanding of the Holy Spirit in his relationship to the Godhead, the creation, the work of reconciliation, the Christian life and the future. It is based on the beliefs that the Holy Spirit is far more important than most of us realise and that we need to take a fresh look at who he is and what he does.

TO THINK ABOUT . . .

Before starting your study of this manual, write down the main points in your current understanding of the Holy Spirit – who he is and what he does.

At the end of your study it will be helpful to see if and how your understanding has changed.

Dorothy Sayers is reputed once to have said:

> There are those who would worship the Father, the Son and the Virgin Mary; those who believe in the Father, the Son and the Holy Scriptures; those who found their faith on the Father, the Son and the Church, and there are those who seem to derive their spiritual power from the Father, the Son and the Minister!

Whether or not she was accurate is not a matter that really concerns us. Her statement is true in so far as it points to a widespread ignorance (until more recent times) of the person and work of the Holy Spirit. The Spirit, it has been claimed with some justification, is the neglected member of the Holy Trinity.

When it comes to the Father, there appears to be little doubt about who he is and what he does.

The Bible begins with the story of the Creator speaking his powerful word into the cosmos; it continues with the righteous yet merciful God who holds a fallen world together despite its sinful rebellion; it focuses on the electing God who calls Abraham and his descendants to be his people; it magnifies the God who sent Jesus as the world's redeemer.

With Jesus, called the Son of God, there also appears to be little difficulty. Having come from God, he revealed him. He lived among us as the Word made flesh, revealing the Father in his words and actions. The love of God was supremely demonstrated in the sacrificial self-offering of Christ on the cross. In this way God in Christ reconciled humankind to himself. These wonderful and mysterious realities were made known to us in the resurrection of Christ from the dead. Through this, Christ was declared to be what he had been from the beginning, the eternal Son of the Father.

But . . . as to the Holy Spirit, many would be able to echo the words of the Ephesian disciples: '. . . we have not even heard that there is a Holy Spirit' (Acts 19:2). It could rightly be objected that this is something of an overstatement. Indeed it is. We need to qualify what has been said and in a moment we will do so. Nevertheless, until recently, what has been claimed is substantially true. The Holy Spirit has not been given the attention he deserves.

TO THINK ABOUT . . .

What did those Ephesian disciples mean? Why might people say the same thing today?

A NEGLECTED PERSON

There are several reasons why the Holy Spirit has been neglected. The following summarises those reasons.

1. A BIBLICAL REASON

The Bible tells of the unfolding drama of God's dealings with the world. It is only in the latter parts of the Bible, particularly in the New Testament, that the Holy Spirit emerges, as it were, from the shadows into the light of day. This is not to say that the Holy Spirit is unknown or unmentioned in the Old Testament. We will see that this is far from the case. Neither does it mean that the Holy Spirit is inactive until later on. He is active from the beginning. But the full significance of who he is and what he does only emerges towards the end of the biblical revelation. Prominence appears to be given to Father and Son before the Holy Spirit. In the order of God's self-revelation, the Holy Spirit only comes into proper focus later.

> ### TO THINK ABOUT . . .
> What references to the Holy Spirit in the Old Testament can you recall? Are you surprised, and if so why, at either how many or how few you think of?

2. A SPIRITUAL REASON

This impression is heightened when we consider a prime aspect of the Holy Spirit's work. According to Jesus:

> When the Counsellor comes, whom I will send to you from the Father, the Spirit of truth who goes out from the Father, he will testify about me (John 15:26).

And again:

> He will bring glory to me by taking from what is mine and making it known to you (John 16:14).

It is not the work of the Holy Spirit to draw attention to himself but to Christ. He teaches us and enables us to confess that Jesus is Lord (1 Cor. 12:3). Of course, the work of the Son is to bring us to the Father (John 14:6). So the work of the Spirit is also to teach us through the Son to call God our Father (Rom. 8:15–16). The point is that the Holy Spirit is concerned to draw our gaze through the Son to the Father.

It should not be surprising, therefore, if he himself stays somewhat in the background. Indeed, the Holy Spirit has been aptly called 'God in his reticence' (T.S. Smail). He does not draw attention to himself but, rather like John the Baptist, points us to the 'Lamb of God who takes away the sin of the world' (John 1:29).

'Look, the Lamb of God . . .'

> ### TO THINK ABOUT . . .
> Is the phrase 'God in his reticence' helpful in your understanding of the Spirit?
>
> In what ways does the parallel with John the Baptist enable you to see why the Holy Spirit might have been neglected?

3. A THEOLOGICAL REASON

Over the years of her history the Christian Church has attempted to think through what she believes. This attempt to think through her faith is called 'theology'. The essential issues occupied much time and effort in the first centuries of her existence. Having experienced salvation in and through Jesus of Nazareth, the crucial issue was to understand correctly exactly who Jesus was and to express how it was that God was present in him, so that certain dangerous misunderstandings could be avoided.

This discussion is not the concern of this particular study guide. It does indicate, however, that in the history of the Church's thinking the study of the Holy Spirit has taken second place to the study of Christ. In theological language, 'Christology' (the doctrine of Christ) has had priority over 'Pneumatology' (the doctrine of the Spirit).

There are good reasons for this. Everything in Christian faith hinges on our understanding of Jesus. Indeed, we cannot even understand who the Spirit is unless we first come to terms with Jesus. But it can be seen that, for quite valid reasons, reflection upon the Spirit has claimed less attention in the history of the Church than reflection upon Christ.

> **TO THINK ABOUT . . .**
> **How do you respond to these three reasons? Do you think they are true? Are there other reasons?**

These three reasons indicate why the Holy Spirit has been neglected in the understanding of the Church. None of these reasons is in itself wrong or sinister. However, honesty compels us to admit that this is not the whole story. At this point we begin to face up to a challenge which will be present throughout this study.

THE LIVING PRESENCE OF THE SPIRIT

The first Christians spoke warmly of the Holy Spirit because for them he was far more than a doctrine. Through the Spirit the love of God had been poured into their hearts (Rom. 8:5). It was through the Spirit that they had first believed and by his power they had been transformed (eg. Acts 11:1–18). They spoke of the Spirit of God because he had for them a dynamic, living reality of whose continuing presence they were abundantly conscious. Nothing can be more obvious: for the early Christians the Holy Spirit was not a theory but a mighty, awe-inspiring and sometimes disruptive power. For them he certainly was the wind that blows wherever he pleases (John 3:8).

Where this is the case, the Holy Spirit will not be neglected but will be spoken of and talked about alongside and in unity with the Father and the Son to whom he testifies. Where it is not the case, he will be neglected. People will begin to say again: 'we have not even heard that there is a Holy Spirit.' Our ignorance of the Holy Spirit has more than a little to do with the fact that, unlike the early Christians, many present-day believers have little awareness of the Spirit's presence and power. We cannot rest content with this state of affairs. Unless this study is directed towards the renewing of a true and living experience of God the Father, through the Son in the Holy Spirit, it will prove to be of little value.

> **TO THINK ABOUT . . .**
> **What difference should it make to study the Holy Spirit not merely as an aspect of Christian doctrine but as a dynamic living reality?**

A RECENT GROWTH OF INTEREST

At this point we need to qualify the claim that the Holy Spirit has been neglected. From time to time in church history some Christians have emphasised the role of the Spirit, but this emphasis has never been so widespread among the churches as in the last thirty years, when there has been a positive explosion of interest in the Spirit. A neglected area has become a topic on everybody's lips. Several factors account for this.

TO THINK ABOUT . . .

In what ways has the renewal movement affected:

a) your own life?
b) the life of your church?

If you consider those affects were negative, why do you think this was the case?

THE CHARISMATIC MOVEMENT

The most obvious factor has been the growth of the charismatic renewal movement. Since the early 1960s a new awareness of the Spirit and his gifts has been awakened within the historic churches of the Christian denominations and within newer, independent groups. This is a movement of major historical importance. Renewed experience of the Holy Spirit has inevitably led to renewed reflection on him. This has particularly been seen in an examination of the biblical texts (especially 1 Corinthians 12 and 14) referring to the gifts of the Spirit which (it is believed) are being newly appropriated.

TO THINK ABOUT . . .

Why did renewed reflection on the Spirit follow and not precede renewed experience of him?

Part of our concern in this study must be therefore to address the questions raised by the renewal movement and to do so in a way which is fair and balanced. A major concern of this study will also be to show the full range of the Holy Spirit's work, in case we fall into the trap of thinking that one aspect of the Spirit's work is the whole. One danger of the renewal movement is that it might restrict the Spirit's work to one area (specifically Christian experience), while missing altogether the breadth of his activity in other realms, such as in the realm of politics and human society.

THEOLOGICAL QUESTIONING

A further factor in the new atmosphere has been a general questioning and particularly a desire to explain more fully the manner of God's presence in the world at large as well as in the church. If the world and all that is in it is truly the Lord's, then we need to find a way of understanding how it is all related to the God who rules and sustains all. This need is made the more obvious because increased awareness of global human experience makes it increasingly difficult for Christians to imagine, as sometimes they have, that God is somehow restricted to the church. God is Lord of all life, and understanding the Holy Spirit as the one who relates all of life to its source enables us to see not only the church but all the world in this light.

EASTERN ORTHODOX THEOLOGY

Openness to Orthodoxy has been a third factor in this reawakened consciousness. This may seem odd, but increased interaction with other theological traditions, made possible by the modern world, opens up new avenues. The Eastern Orthodox tradition has tended to place a greater emphasis than Western theology on the Holy Spirit. In fact, the great split which took place in 1054 C.E. (Common Era) between the churches of East and West was largely due to this issue.

The more ecumenical climate of recent years makes it possible to learn from others, and the prominence given to the Spirit in the East is one of the areas where this may happen. The debate is complex. Suffice it to say at this point that, whereas the West has linked the work of the Spirit very closely to the saving work of Christ, the East has wanted to conceive of his work more broadly.

Together these factors have created a new climate for examining the person and work of the Spirit of God and this study guide aims:

1. To examine what the Bible teaches concerning the Holy Spirit and to see why it is that the Christian Church has honoured him as the Lord and Giver of Life.

2. To seek to understand the full breadth of the Spirit's work within God, the creation, the Church, the Christian believer and human society.

3. To explore the best ways in which the work of the Holy Spirit in Christians may be described so that we may express his work in us and in others accurately and helpfully.

UNIT 1

The Spirit – God on the Inside

THIS STUDY BEGINS AT THE END! Rather than collect all the evidence of what the Bible says about the Spirit and then come to conclusions concerning what it means, we will begin with the conclusion already reached by generations of Christians before us. We will then seek to show how that conclusion is justified by testing it against the evidence that the Bible gives.

THINGS MOST SURELY BELIEVED

The Christian church has affirmed as part of its creed that:

The Holy Spirit is truly and fully God. The Spirit shares with the Father and the Son the fullness of deity. He is not an inferior deity of another kind, nor is he an inferior part of the one true deity. He is himself fully and truly God, as the Spirit of the Father and the Son in the Triune God.

The Holy Spirit is someone and not something. He is not an impersonal force nor merely the projection of God's power into the world. He is himself fully personal and, within the tri-unity of God, is as distinctively personal as the Father and the Son.

In saying this we recognise that any language used of God must be inadequate. It is like trying to capture the immensity of the ocean in a teacup. Yet this is the kind of language that the Bible leads us to use of God. It may be inadequate but it is not inaccurate. This is the language we have already used in the Introduction.

We have clearly acknowledged that the Spirit is the Spirit of God and we have spoken of him using personal pronouns, as 'he' and 'him' rather than 'it'. We have already assumed, therefore, and will go on assuming, that the words of the Nicene creed are true:

> **And I believe in the Holy Spirit,**
> **the Lord, the Giver of Life,**
> **who proceeds from the Father and the Son,**
> **who with the Father and the Son together**
> **is worshipped and glorified,**
> **who spoke by the prophets.**

TO THINK ABOUT . . .
Recognising the strict inaccuracy of a child who gathers a cupful of sea water and exclaims with delight: 'I've got the ocean', what images, pictures and models most help you to understand and explain the Holy Spirit – to feel you have grasped who he is?

This is the faith of the church. We are beginning at the end in the sense that we are already operating with certain conclusions about the Holy Spirit before we have examined the biblical evidence about him. It is impossible to avoid this.

> **TO THINK ABOUT . . .**
> How much have your ideas about the Holy Spirit been shaped by what you have been taught? From what sources (e.g. parents, preachers, books, friends) have you gained your ideas?

The large majority of those who attempt this study will already be committed Christians who gladly affirm the faith that has been handed on to them. But it is necessary to show along the way why it is that these conclusions have been reached and why they are still valid. This will involve examining the witness to the Holy Spirit in the Bible and this is the task we now begin.

> **TO THINK ABOUT . . .**
> In what other areas of life do you believe and trust before you fully understand?

GOD ON THE INSIDE OF THE CHRISTIAN

We have entitled this unit 'God on the Inside'. The Holy Spirit is God at work on the inside of the Christian believer. In the words of one theologian, he is 'God at his closest to us'. The Father is God above us and over us (Isaiah 6:6); the Son is God with us and among us (Matt. 1:23); the Holy Spirit is God in us, on the inside. Jesus said:

> You know him, for he lives with you and *will be in you* (John 14:17).

This is why Paul could talk about Christians being:

> God's temple and that God's Spirit lives in you (1 Cor. 3:16).

Of course, because the Spirit is God's Spirit, this also means that through the Holy Spirit the Father and the Son live within us. Again, Jesus said:

> If anyone loves me, he will obey my teaching. My Father will love him and we will come to him and make our home with him (John 14:23).

The Father and the Son come and make their home in Christians through the Holy Spirit: God on the inside.

> **TO THINK ABOUT . . .**
> What are some of the practical differences in your life since coming to know that the Holy Spirit of God lives within you?

CREATING FELLOWSHIP WITH GOD

To grasp this is crucial for this reason: What God's Spirit does in the world and in the church shows us clearly who the Spirit is and what he does *within God himself*. What he does in believers is characteristic of who and what the Spirit is.

This can be expressed slightly differently along these lines. In 2 Cor. 13:14 we find the well known words: 'May the grace of the Lord Jesus Christ, and the love of God, and the fellowship of the Holy Spirit be with you all.' As grace is a prime characteristic of the person and work of Christ, and love is a prime characteristic of the person and work of the Father, so *fellowship* is characteristic of the person and work of the Holy Spirit. The Holy Spirit creates and produces fellowship. He is the bond, the power that connects each believer with Christ and through him with the Father. Through Christ we have access to the Father *by one Spirit* (Eph. 2:18).

Used by permission of the Bible Society.

TO THINK ABOUT . . .
How do you feel about Annie Vallotton's illustration? Do its images and symbols help you appreciate more fully the Holy Spirit's unifying work?

CREATING FELLOWSHIP AMONG BELIEVERS

In the same way the Spirit is the bond between Christians. 'Make every effort to keep the unity of the Spirit through the bond of peace' (Eph. 4:3).

The Spirit is the Spirit of unity, of fellowship, the one who forges relationship. This work is characteristic of who he is and what he does in the world. This is because it is also characteristic of who the Spirit is and what he does within the being of God himself. In other words, what he does in space and in time reveals what he does in eternity in God. Within God, the Spirit is the Spirit of fellowship, the dynamic bond of love between the Father and the Son.

TO THINK ABOUT . . .
Recall examples of broken fellowship within your church. In the light of the paragraph above, how might those hindrances to fellowship be overcome?

ON THE INSIDE OF GOD

UNRESTRICTED ACCESS

Is it possible to talk about the inside of God? To do so would seem foolish were it not the case that we have 'access to the Father by one Spirit'.

In the Old Testament the people of God were made aware that they must keep their distance from God. His holiness and their sin combined to keep people at a distance. At Mount Sinai the people were warned to keep away from the Lord 'or he will break out against them' (Ex. 19:24). Even when the tabernacle was built, the people were still unable to approach God too closely. Only the High Priest was allowed to enter the Holy of Holies and only once a year (Heb. 9:7 –8).

Yet when Jesus made atonement for sins, the curtain of the temple was torn in two (Mark 15:38). In this a profound spiritual statement is being made. Unrestricted access to God has been

opened up for those who believe in Christ. Those who were far away have been brought near through the blood of Christ (Eph. 2:13 –18).

GOD'S UNITY IN VARIETY

From the outside God is one. But those who have been reconciled to God have access to his inner being. From the inside we perceive that God is still one, but this unity is a unity in variety. God has three ways of being God. He is God as the Father, as the Son and as the Holy Spirit. The unity of God is a three-dimensional unity. We know this to be so because God has revealed himself in this way. He has shown us who he is in his work, in the coming of his Son and the giving of his Spirit. From his work we are able to draw accurate conclusions as to who he is within himself. This 'threeness' in God is known in the church's language as 'Trinity'.

Perhaps some technical theological language is appropriate and forgiveable here. Christian theology has usually made a distinction between the 'economic' Trinity (that is: Father, Son and Spirit as they are seen through their activity in the world) and the 'ontological' or 'immanent' Trinity (that is: God as he is in himself, within his own eternal being).

The key point is that the economic and the ontological Trinity are identical. The way God shows himself in the world is how he actually is in himself. There is no other God apart from this God, who shows himself to be Father, Son and Spirit.

> ## TO THINK ABOUT . . .
> **Pause until you have grasped this point. Why is it an important point to make? What difference does it make?**

GOD IS A LOVING COMMUNITY

This understanding of God is one of the most dynamic and exciting aspects of the Christian faith. It means that, truly understood, God is not some far off, isolated being. He is a loving community of divine persons who has his being in perfect, self-giving love.

Within God's threefold, three-in-one existence, the Holy Spirit is the Spirit of the Father and of the Son. He is the dynamic, loving bond who expresses their unity. On the inside of God he does the same kind of thing that he does on the inside of the believer. He creates fellowship. He unites in love. He enables Father and Son to be in perfect harmony with each other in himself. Because he first of all fulfils this within God, he is able to fulfil the same within those who believe.

'The Trinity' by William Blake.   By permission of the British Library

> ## TO THINK ABOUT . . .
> **What is your response to Blake's picture? In what ways may it be a helpful attempt to describe God as a loving community?**

DESCRIBING THE SPIRIT'S WORK

These themes have been taken up by Christian thinkers and we shall look here at one ancient and one modern approach.

AUGUSTINE

Augustine (354–430), Bishop of Hippo in North Africa and one of the most influential theologians ever, described the Holy Trinity in terms of Lover, Beloved and Love. By this he meant that the Father is the Lover, the source of love, the Son is Beloved, the one who is loved, and the Holy Spirit is Love, the bond or 'nexus' of love between them.

This analogy runs the danger of making the Holy Spirit less than personal, but in its own way it is attempting to be true to the 'fellowship of the Holy Spirit'.

JOHN TAYLOR

Bishop John V. Taylor developed the theme more recently in a book entitled *The Go-Between God*. The Holy Spirit is 'the current of communication' between the Father and the Son, eternally holding each in awareness of the other. He is the 'Go-Between God', the bond of union between Father and Son, truly God and truly personal.

These are helpful trains of thought, not least because they bring God alive for us. God exists in dynamic, creative relationship. He is the Living God whose being overflows with love and joy. It is this overflow of the divine life which has gone out from God to bring the universe into being and to bring creatures such as ourselves into fellowship with himself, breaking down the barriers which we erect, filling us also with the fullness of life which is his own.

> **TO THINK ABOUT . . .**
>
> **Does the term 'Go-Between God' help or hinder your understanding of the Holy Spirit's person and work? Why do you answer as you do?**

IS THE DESCRIPTION RIGHT?

So far so good! But here we come to a major question. Have we got it right? Is God really like this? The quick answer is that only God knows! But because Christians believe that God has revealed himself in Jesus Christ and that the Bible bears witness to this self-revelation, we must go on to ask, does the Bible teach this understanding of God and specifically of the Holy Spirit?

Because our concern is with the Holy Spirit, we will limit ourselves here to examining some of the evidence concerning the Spirit.

EVIDENCE FOR THE SPIRIT'S DEITY

The Holy Spirit is truly God. The truth of this statement rests on several kinds of biblical evidence as follows:

THE HOLY SPIRIT AND GOD INTERCHANGEABLE

References to the Holy Spirit and God are made which are interchangeable. For instance, Acts 5:3–4 records the incident with Ananias and Sapphira. In v.3 Peter says: 'You have lied to the Holy Spirit', and in v.4 this becomes: 'You have not lied to men but to God.' To lie to the Spirit is to lie to God.

Similarly, in 1 Cor. 3:16 Paul says: 'Don't you know that you are God's temple and that God's Spirit lives in you?' To be indwelt by the Spirit is to be indwelt by God.

upon you, and the power of the Most High will overshadow you';

omniscience – 1 Cor. 2:10–11 'The Spirit searches all things, even the deep things of God. For who among men knows the thought of a man except the man's spirit within him? In the same way no-one knows the thoughts of God except the Spirit of God';

eternity – Heb. 9:14 '. . . who through the eternal Spirit offered himself . . .'.

PERFORMS DIVINE WORKS

The Holy Spirit is said to perform works which are clearly seen to be the works of God. These include **creation** (Gen. 1:2, Ps. 104:30), the **resurrection of Christ** (Rom. 8:11) and **inspiration** (2 Tim. 3:16, 2 Pet. 1:2). Clearly the Spirit is seen to be the agent of God at work in the world to such an extent that he is to be equated with God. 'Now the Lord is the Spirit and where the Spirit of the Lord is there is freedom' (2 Cor. 3:17).

> *TO THINK ABOUT . . .*
>
> **The incident in Acts 5 reminds us that the Spirit is always present. God is with us permanently. How should that affect our speech?**
>
> **In what other ways can we lie to the Holy Spirit?**

> *TO THINK ABOUT . . .*
>
> **Is this just a way of talking about the active presence of God within the world or is more intended?**
>
> **Before moving on, consider how important it is to ascribe distinct personality to the Holy Spirit.**

GIVEN THE ATTRIBUTES OF GOD

What can be attributed to God can be attributed to the Spirit. This includes:

power – Lk. 1:35 'The Holy Spirit will come

EVIDENCE FOR THE SPIRIT'S PERSONALITY

The Holy Spirit is personal. This is not to say that he is a person in the limited and individualist sense that humans are, but that in his divine manner of being he possesses the kind of personal being of which human being is a mere reflection. This finds expression in the New Testament in several ways.

> *TO THINK ABOUT . . .*
>
> **What would you describe as the chief marks of being 'personal' and of being human?**
>
> **What are the differences between being personal and being human?**

USE OF PERSONAL PRONOUNS

In Greek, the word 'pneuma' (Spirit) is a neuter noun and should take a neuter pronoun (it). It is significant, therefore, that on occasions, and in direct defiance of the rules of Greek grammar, the word is actually given a personal (masculine) pronoun (he).

This is true of John 16:13–14 ('But when he, the Spirit of truth, comes, he will . . .') and probably also of Eph. 1:14 ('. . . who is a deposit guaranteeing . . .'), although here there are two possible readings of the original text. The point is that the rules of grammar have to be bent in order to express the full reality of the Spirit. The rules must be bent in this specific way to be true to the personal reality of the Spirit.

> **TO THINK ABOUT . . .**
> What difference does it make if we accept that the Holy Spirit is not an impersonal force (an 'it') but a Person?

DESCRIPTIONS OF THE SPIRIT'S PERSONAL ROLE

The Holy Spirit is said to act in ways which are distinctly personal. This is particularly clear in the Gospel of John where, in referring to the Counsellor (Paraclete) who would come, Jesus says the Spirit will teach and remind the disciples (14:26), not testify about himself (15:26), convict the world of sin (16:8) and not bring glory to himself (16:14). These are all the activities of a personal agent.

The impression is intensified when Jesus makes it clear that his own personal presence with his disciples is continued through the Holy Spirit (14:16–18). It would be impossible to speak in this way of a power that was less than personal.

PERSONAL CHARACTERISTICS ASCRIBED TO THE SPIRIT

The Spirit is spoken of as possessing personal qualities. This is true in the active sense: he is said to possess intelligence and knowledge (John 14:26), decision and will (1 Cor. 12:11) and emotions (Eph. 4:30), the qualities which cumulatively define and describe personal existence. It

is true in the passive sense: the Spirit can be lied to (Acts 5:3–4), grieved (Eph. 4:30) and resisted (Acts 7:51).

> **TO THINK ABOUT . . .**
> Hermas, a second-century Christian writer, called the Spirit 'a cheerful Spirit' (the Greek word 'hilaron' which gives us our word 'hilarity'). In what ways is it possible to grieve this cheerful person?
>
> Note how Isaiah 63:10 also speaks of the Spirit of God being grieved.

TRULY PERSONAL – TRULY GOD

These references are by no means exhaustive. In the course of this study we shall have opportunity to note many others. But enough has been said by now to confirm the Christian understanding of the Spirit as truly personal and truly God. It comes as no surprise, therefore, to note the outrage which is felt by Jesus when the works of the Holy Spirit are denigrated:

> Anyone who speaks a word against the Son of Man will be forgiven, but anyone who speaks against the Holy Spirit will not be forgiven, either in this age or in the age to come' (Matt. 12:32).

According to Jesus, to speak against the Holy Spirit is blasphemy. In the mind of the Son of God, the honour of the Spirit of God is of paramount importance.

> **TO THINK ABOUT . . .**
> Review this evidence for the Spirit's personality. What conclusions do you draw from it? Are there other conclusions which could be drawn?

EVIDENCE FOR THE SPIRIT'S ROLE WITHIN THE TRINITARIAN LIFE OF GOD

Before completing this unit we need to review a further area concerning the relationship of the Spirit to the Father and the Son.

On two significant occasions the Holy Spirit is mentioned in the closest possible connection with the Father and the Son.

THE BAPTISMAL FORMULA

In the baptismal formula mentioned in Matt. 28:19 the disciples are commissioned to baptise 'in the name of the Father and of the Son and of the Holy Spirit'. Here are expressed:

the **unity** of God, since there is one name in which we are baptised;

the **triunity** of God, since there are three names within the one name;

the **equality** of the persons in God, since all three persons are mentioned;

the **economy** within God, since the Father is mentioned first, the Son second, the Spirit third, corresponding to the economy of God's self-revelation.

'I baptise you in the name of the Father, Son and Holy Spirit.'

THE GRACE

In 2 Cor. 13:14 we find the equally well known verses: 'May the grace of our Lord Jesus Christ and the love of God and the fellowship of the Holy Spirit be with you all.' Here also we find the same truths, although expressed differently.

There is a **unity** of persons, since the divine blessing comes from Father, Son and Spirit;

there are **triunity** and **equality**, since the persons are each and together the source of divine blessing;

there is **economy**, since the Father is designated as 'God'. This does not deny that Son and Spirit are also God but that the Father is the source of their deity. They have their being from his.

> ### TO THINK ABOUT . . .
> **What guaranteed blessings from God are affirmed when with other Christians you share the words of the grace?**

FURTHER INSIGHTS ON THE INSIDE OF GOD

The evidence of the verses above needs to be placed against that of references to the Spirit as the 'Spirit of God' (*eg.* 1 Cor. 2:11, Phil. 3:3) and the 'Spirit of Christ' (*eg.* Phil. 1:19, 1 Pet. 1:11). When it is further considered that both the Father and the Son are said to give, send or pour out the Spirit (John 14:16; Acts 2:33), we can see why several further conclusions have been drawn about the relationship between Father, Son and Spirit.

(i) Because the Father is the Father he is regarded as the eternal source of the Son and the Spirit. He is the fountain and origin of deity.

(ii) Whereas the Son, because he is the Son, may be said to be 'eternally begotten' from the Father, the Spirit is to be thought of as eternally 'proceeding' or 'going out' from the Father and from the Son. This is suggested by the general way in which the New Testament speaks of the Spirit's work and particularly by John 15:26 '. . . the Spirit of truth who goes out from the Father . . .' Thus the Spirit is not another Son. He has his own unique identity and his own way of relating within the Trinity.

(iii) Because the Spirit is the Spirit of fellowship, and because he is the Spirit of the Father and the Son, the Spirit may be thought of as the bond of fellowship between Father and Son, the current of loving communication between them.

If these things are true, the picture of God which emerges is exciting: the Living God, full of life in himself and active among us by his Spirit.

TO THINK ABOUT . . .

Do you find this picture of God as exciting as is suggested? If so, why?

What difference does this way of thinking about God make to our understanding of his being present in the world?

ASSIGNMENT 1

How the Spirit has been understood

For this assignment you will need to obtain a modern service book such as the Anglican Alternative Service Book, a traditional hymnbook of any kind and a collection of more modern songs.

Using the materials you have to hand, research the following areas:

1. How has the church confessed her understanding of the Holy Spirit in the Apostles' Creed and the Nicene Creed? What picture of the Spirit do you see emerging?

2. What do the more traditional hymnbooks of the church have to tell us about the Spirit in their sections on the Holy Trinity and the Holy Spirit?

3. Examine the more recent songs and seek to determine in what ways *a.* they reveal the same understanding and *b.* they give evidence of changes in emphasis?

Summarise the results of your research in a short (no more than 1000 words) article for your church newsletter entitled 'Is the Holy Spirit who we think he is?'

UNIT 2

The Spirit and Creation

IN UNIT 1 our concern was to understand the Holy Spirit as truly personal and truly God. In the rest of this study-guide we are concerned to understand the breadth and the nature of the Spirit's work as this is revealed in Scripture. At this point we encounter head on a difficulty that we will be seeking to address throughout our study.

YOUR GOD IS TOO SMALL

Just as Christians can have a God who is too small, so they can have an idea of the Spirit which is too small. We make the Spirit of God too small when, for instance, we restrict the scope of his activity to salvation and to the church.

TO THINK ABOUT . . .
In what ways do you see the Holy Spirit locked-in as it were to churchy concerns and matters relating to personal salvation?

We need to see first of all that the Holy Spirit is the Spirit of creation. He is the power of God at work, bringing the world into being and holding it together. If the work of the Spirit is particular-

ly characterised by 'fellowship', so that he can be called the 'Go-Between God', it leads us to realise that it is the Spirit of God who holds the world together. He is the power of God present and active in the world, so that it can truly be said: 'For in him we live and move and have our being' (Acts 17:28). The biblical understanding of creation, then, is as much to do with God sustaining, upholding and acting in providence towards what he has made as with starting the world off in the first place. Our concern in this unit is: What is the role of the Holy Spirit in creation?

TO THINK ABOUT . . .
Before reading on, what would be your immediate answer to this question?

THE SPIRIT'S ROLE IN CREATION

To understand this question it is possible to proceed in two ways.

THE WAY OF THEOLOGICAL DEDUCTION

It is possible to deduce the role of the Spirit in creation from the statements already made about the Trinity. The work of Father, Son and Spirit in the world should not be divided. What the Father and the Son do is also what the Spirit does. It is essential to recognise that there are

distinct relations within the Trinity and that Father, Son and Spirit may be said to fulfil differing and distinctive roles. But when it comes to the work of God in the world, although certain activities are specifically focused in particular persons of the Trinity, the other persons share in those activities as well.

Thus, although atonement is supremely the work of the Son, it is also that of Father and Spirit. Although conviction of sin is a work of the Spirit, it would be wrong to say it is not also the work of the Son and the Father.

When it comes to creation, the work of creation is supremely that of the Father, but in this work the Son and the Spirit share. Putting it slightly differently: If the Spirit really is God, then he must also share in the work of creation since God is the Creator. It should come as no surprise, therefore, to find that the Bible clearly confirms this deduction.

However, we have not yet finished with our theological deductions. There is a further point. In the New Testament, creation is seen as the work of the Father through the Son. The Son of God is spoken of as the Word of God by whom all things have been made. This is particularly clear in John 1:3.

> Through him all things were made; without him nothing was made that has been made.

Christ is therefore the creative word spoken by the Father of which we read in Genesis 1, when it is repeatedly recorded: 'And God said . . .' (vv.3, 6, 9, 14, 20, 24). But for a word to be spoken, breath is required. Here we see the involvement of the Father in speaking the creative word, of the Son in being the creative word which is spoken and of the Spirit in being the means (i.e. the breath) whereby the creative word is uttered.

> By the word of the LORD were the heavens made, their starry host by the breath of his mouth (Psa. 33:6).

We now pursue a second path.

THE WAY OF BIBLICAL TESTIMONY

The deductions that we have already made are confirmed by the biblical witness.

Explicit confirmation. A small but significant collection of verses ties the Spirit very closely to creation. For instance, in Genesis 1:2 we find the words:

> . . . and the Spirit of God was hovering over the waters.

Here at the beginning of the creation narrative we are introduced to the Spirit hovering over the formless and empty chaos which has been called into being by God. Out of this raw material the creative word of God then proceeds to shape the ordered world which we know. The implication is that the Spirit is intimately involved in this.

That this was indeed the faith of Israel is suggested by Elihu's confession in the book of Job:

> The Spirit of God has made me, the breath of the Almighty gives me life (Job 33:4).

The involvement of the Spirit in creation and in the sustaining of all things is well expressed in Psalm 104:30:

> When you send your Spirit they are created, and you renew the face of the earth.

This involvement of the Spirit extends to the universal presence of God by his Spirit in the world, so that there is no escaping him nor is there anything hidden from him:

> Where can I go from your Spirit? Where can I flee from your presence? If I go up to the heavens, you are there; if I make my bed in the depths, you are there . . . My frame was not hidden from you . . . (Psa. 139:7–8, 15).

Implicit confirmation. The explicit testimonies are strengthened by some implicit confirmation. In the Old Testament the Hebrew word *ruach* means spirit, wind and breath. The word itself occurs 378 times in the Old Testament with at least one of these meanings.

In the famous passage about the dry bones in Ezekiel 37:1–14, it is evident that all three possible meanings are being used in close proximity. The wind blows on the bones and puts breath in them, just as the Spirit of God will come upon his people and give them life. It is as if the Spirit is the breath of God activating and moving his creation, creating and sustaining life (Job 32:8, Gen. 2:7).

> In his hand is the life of every creature and the breath of all mankind (Job 12:10).

TO THINK ABOUT . . .
What does it mean for every day living that we depend on God for our daily breath?

The Spirit of God is as essential to life as the wind that blows upon the face of the earth and the breath that activates the living creatures within it. Indeed, the living universe is sustained and upheld from moment to moment by the presence of the creative Spirit who breathes through all creation. The Spirit who is the divine Go-Between within the Godhead is the same as the relating and connecting power which holds the universe together, the current of communication binding all things together.

All of this points to the closeness of the Spirit of God. It is impossible with this understanding of the Spirit to think of God as being distant and far off. He is as close as the breath or the wind. It is equally impossible to conceive of the Spirit in a narrow or restricted way. He is in all life and all of creation. Everything that is has its being in God. His Spirit undergirds and upholds all. Whenever we think about the Spirit we must think big thoughts.

TO THINK ABOUT . . .
Before reading on, suggest some examples of how the point made in this last paragraph gives your life a greater sense of unity. What areas of life have you tended to see as having nothing to do with God?

THE SPIRIT AT WORK IN ALL LIFE

The importance of all this for the Christian should now be clear. As the Creator Spirit, the Holy Spirit is not confined to the church. It is true as we shall see that the church is in a particular sense the dwelling place of the Spirit. But we must reckon with his presence in all the other activities of human life. He holds in his hands all the life and all the ways of humankind, even where he is not honoured (Dan. 5:23). This may be summarised in the following statements, drawing on the witness of the Old Testament, the understanding of which is essential for the New Testament:

MOULDING CREATION AND GIVING LIFE

The Spirit moulds creation into shape and gives life to all created things. This is indicated by what has been said already.

TO THINK ABOUT . . .

What examples from the world and all that is in it illustrate for you most clearly the creative work of the Holy Spirit?

CONTROLLING NATURE AND HISTORY

The Spirit controls the course of nature and history. Writing of the falcons, Isaiah of Jerusalem says:

> None of these will be missing, not one will lack her mate. For it is his mouth that has given the order, and his Spirit will gather them together (Isa. 34:16).

In asserting the Lord's sovereignty over the nations, Isaiah 40:7 reads:

> The grass withers and the flowers fall, because the breath [ruach] of the Lord blows on them.

Through the Spirit, God exercises his rule over the nations.

ENRICHING HUMANKIND WITH GIFTS

The Spirit enriches the life of humankind by pouring out his gifts. This may be seen in two particular ways:

The Spirit enables creative achievement. There is clear evidence that the creative abilities

I have given skill to all the craftsmen.

TO THINK ABOUT . . .

Through what skills, crafts, hobbies and talents does the Spirit enable you and those close to you to share his creative achievement?

of humanity should be seen as the gracious gifts of the Spirit of God. For example, in Exodus 31:1–11 and 35:30–35 we read of Bezalel and Oholiab being equipped to construct the Tabernacle and its furnishings:

> See I have chosen Bezalel, son of Uri . . . and I have filled him with the Spirit of God, with skill, ability and knowledge in all kinds of crafts . . . Also I have given skill to all the craftsmen to make everything I have commanded you (31:2–3, 6).

Much later, after the Exile, when the time came to rebuild the temple, the people are reminded through Haggai:

> This is what I covenanted with you when you came out of Egypt. And my Spirit remains among you (Haggai 2:5).

These words remind the people that the creative abilities they need for rebuilding the temple remain among them.

The Spirit bestows on individuals wisdom and leadership abilities. That the Spirit equips people for leadership emerges as a constant theme in the Old Testament. This is true, for example, of Joseph (Gen. 41:38), Moses (Numbers 11:17), Othniel (Judges 3:10), Gideon (Judges 6:34), Samson (Judges 13:25), Saul (1 Sam. 10:10), David (1 Sam. 16:13) and of the hoped for Messiah (Isa. 11:1–15, 42:1–4). The Spirit who equips for leadership is the Spirit of wisdom and understanding (Isa. 11:2, Dan. 2:21, 5:14).

TO THINK ABOUT . . .

Read Numbers 10:11–17. Why is efficient administration so often talked about in disparaging terms? Why is it sometimes regarded as less spiritual ministry than other aspects of leadership?

These aspects of the Spirit's work relate to the people of God, so it might be thought that they are not evidence of the presence and work of the Holy Spirit generally enabling creative achievement and bestowing wisdom and leadership ability on mankind. This would be an unnecessary assumption.

We need to remember that God is the giver of every good gift (James 1:17) and it is through the Spirit, the active presence of God in his world, that these gifts must come. It is certainly true that the people of God are distinct. The prophet Amos makes this point clearly when he gives God's word:

> You only have I chosen of all the families of the earth (Amos 3:2).

But it is wrong to assume that the Spirit is restricted to God's people. A later word recorded by Amos reads:

> 'Are not you Israelites the same to me as the Cushites?' declares the Lord. 'Did I not bring Israel up from Egypt, the Philistines from Caphtor and the Arameans from Kir?' (9:7).

God is gracious to all the nations and active by his Spirit within their history.

TO THINK ABOUT . . .

What signs of God at work by his Spirit do you currently see in, for example, the lands of Eastern Europe and the Middle East?

DRAWING OUT RESPONSE TO GOD

The Spirit works to draw out response to God from his human creatures. As we shall see, the supreme work of the Spirit is to bring people to know God. This means that the Spirit works to create repentance, faith and obedience: in short, to be the agent of fellowship between God and people.

Primarily we must see this work of the Spirit within his chosen people. The Spirit awakens us to God and causes us to search after him. So the Psalmist can say:

> Create in me a pure heart, O God, and renew a steadfast Spirit within me. Do not cast me from your presence or take your Holy Spirit from me (Psa. 51:10–11).

Ezekiel and Jeremiah can both point to a new day when the Lord would put his Spirit in his people and cause them to obey him from the heart (Ezek. 36:24–32; Jer. 31:31–34).

Furthermore, the Spirit's work in God's people

is a prelude to a greater universal work spoken of by Joel:

> And afterwards I will pour out my Spirit on all people . . . and everyone who calls on the name of the LORD will be saved (Joel 2:28–32).

It is through the Spirit, then, that God is at work creating fellowship with people, in his saving purpose first electing Israel and then the Church, in order that through them his purposes of salvation may be extended throughout the world (Isa. 24:6; 1 Peter 2:9–10). The Spirit who breathes through all creation is the one who enables people to respond to the gracious callings of God.

SUMMARY

The object of this unit has been to broaden our understanding of the Spirit's activity. The Spirit needs to be seen in all of life and all of life needs to be seen in the Spirit. He is the creating and sustaining power of God. Through him the good gifts of God are imparted to us, enriching life, inspiring creativity, enabling response to God and therefore helping us to find true life as persons made by God and for him.

It is tragically true that humans as fallen and sinful creatures have marred the life they have been given and spoiled the creation of which they are stewards. But graciously the Spirit holds us in being, giving us space and time to learn repentance and faith. Our dependence on the Spirit of God is total.

> **TO THINK ABOUT . . .**
>
> How will the content of this unit affect the way you think about:
>
> a) manual crafts and skills?
> b) art?
> c) music?
> d) changes taking place in the political systems of our time?

UNIT 3

The Spirit and Revelation

IN THE PREVIOUS UNIT we began to touch on the work of the Spirit in drawing out from people a response to God. The Spirit makes for fellowship between God and people. Yet it is impossible for such fellowship to become a reality unless human beings see that God is, and that he makes demands on us. It is here, therefore, that we must speak about revelation: the action God takes to make himself known to us, his self-disclosure to humanity.

It is part of the Spirit's work to be the means whereby the word of God comes to us and is heard by us. This is consistent with the understanding we have already outlined of the Spirit as the 'current of communication' between Father and Son. This same Spirit opens up the channels of communication between the Father and ourselves through the Son.

The Spirit's involvement in the work of revelation is the subject to which we now turn.

TO THINK ABOUT . . .
Recall particular times when through prayer, preaching or Bible study you have experienced moments of 'revelation'. How would you describe such moments and how would you see the Spirit at work on those occasions?

THE SPIRIT AND PROPHECY

That the Holy Spirit enables people to speak from God is a clear theme in Scripture. This is most obvious in 2 Peter 1:21:

> For prophecy never had its origin in the will of man, but men spoke from God as they were carried along by the Holy Spirit.

The sense here is of being carried along by a wave and this is not an inappropriate way of describing the prophetic experience in both Old Testament and New Testament. It takes varied forms as God speaks 'at many times and in various ways' (Heb. 1:1). We shall examine at this point the witness of both testaments.

THE OLD TESTAMENT

From early on in Israel's history the Spirit is associated with prophecy. So we read of Balaam:

> . . . the Spirit of God came upon him and he uttered his oracle (Num. 24:2–3).

When the time comes to anoint Saul as King over Israel, Samuel tells him that, in confirmation, he will encounter a procession of prophets and:

> The Spirit of the LORD will come upon you in power, and you will prophesy with them (1 Sam. 10:6, see also 1 Sam. 19:23–24).

The kind of experience referred to here can only be described as 'ecstatic', as Saul is overcome by a power greater than himself. King David is reported as saying:

> The Spirit of the LORD spoke through me; his word was on my tongue (2 Sam. 23:2).

TO THINK ABOUT . . .
Does what is described here have any relation to what is experienced today as the gift of prophecy?

These early prophetic experiences become characteristic of the later prophetic movement interpreting the ways of God to his covenant people. In the case of Ezekiel, the revelation of God comes both in vision and word (see Ezek. 2:2, 3:12–14, 11:1, 5, 24, 37:1 etc). The prophet proclaims in Isaiah 61:1–4:

> The Spirit of the Sovereign LORD is on me, because the LORD has annointed me to preach good news to the poor.

These words are echoed by Micah:

> But as for me, I am filled with power, with the Spirit of the LORD, and with justice and might, to declare to Jacob his transgression . . . (Mic. 3:8).

TO THINK ABOUT . . .
Why is it essential to be filled with the Spirit before you denounce evil?

It was the Holy Spirit who enabled the prophets to be bearers of the word of the Lord. He enlightened their minds to perceive in the events of history a depth of meaning hidden from others. Through dreams and visions they perceived what was in the heart of the God of the covenant, and the Spirit pressed the word of the Lord on them with such urgency that they were compelled to speak for him. They were 'carried along by the Holy Spirit'.

THE NEW TESTAMENT

Against this Old Testament background it comes as no surprise to find similar prophetic experiences in the New Testament. In the tradition of the Old Testament prophets, the word of God comes to John the Baptist (Luke 3:2), a man 'filled with the Holy Spirit even from birth' (Luke 1:15). With prophetic insight he sees the Spirit of God descending and resting on Jesus (John 1:33). After his baptism Jesus enters into a prophetic ministry, in fulfilment of the words from Isaiah already quoted: 'The Spirit of the Lord is upon me' (Luke 4:18–19; cf. Isa. 61:1–2). On the day of Pentecost, Peter sees the fulfilment of the prophecy of Joel concerning the outpouring of the Spirit in the last days. The result will be:

> Your sons and daughters will prophesy, your young men will see visions, your old men will dream dreams (Acts 2:17–18; cf. Joel 2:28–32).

The church after Pentecost is marked by this prophetic constraint. We read of the prophet Agabus who proclaims: 'The Holy Spirit says . . .' (Acts 21:10–11). The prophetic experience is in evidence in Corinth and is seen by Paul as a gift of the Spirit to be desired because of its usefulness in building up the people of God (1 Cor. 12:7–11, 14:1–5). The prophecies of John the Seer were given in visions when he was 'in the Spirit' on the Lord's Day (Rev. 1:10).

From this selection of evidence we are able to see that the Spirit brings to God's people the revelation of God. He is the means by which God gives himself to his people, enabling them to know what is in his heart and mind.

TO THINK ABOUT . . .
Are there ways by which God 'speaks' to people today, other than through words?

THE SPIRIT AND SCRIPTURE

An extension of the Spirit's inspiration of prophecy is his inspiration of Scripture. The Scriptures are, in large measure, the collected oracles of the prophets or prophetically edited writings interpreting Israel's history. Within the variety of Scripture there are however writings which fit into neither of these categories. Nevertheless, speaking with reference to the Old Testament, 2 Timothy 3:16–17 asserts:

> All Scripture is God-breathed and is useful for teaching, rebuking, correcting and training in righteousness, so that the man of God may be thoroughly equipped for every good work.

These words have commonly been extended to the New Testament on the basis of John 14:26 and 16:13, where Jesus tells the apostles that the Spirit will guide them into all truth. When this is combined with 1 Corinthians 2:13, where Paul claims to have taught the truth in 'words taught by the Spirit', the conclusion is that both testaments are the inspired word of God.

> *TO THINK ABOUT...*
> **What does the phrase 'the Spirit's inspiration of Scripture' mean to you? How does your answer affect your view of the Bible's authority?**

It is not the purpose of this study manual to go in detail into the meaning of inspiration or its implications. It is sufficient here to indicate that, as the Spirit was at work inspiring the prophets, so he was at work calling into being the Scriptures as we now possess them. God by his Spirit has invested himself in the words of Scripture, so that they bear witness to the central Word which is Jesus Christ himself (Luke 24:25–27; John 5:39–40). The result of his activity is that the Bible we now possess is:

> useful for teaching, rebuking, correcting and training in righteousness (2 Tim. 3:16).

> *TO THINK ABOUT...*
> **How is the Holy Spirit using the Bible to accomplish these four things in your life?**

Implicit in this is the fact that the Scriptures, by reason of their inspiration, are altogether reliable in fulfilling their central purpose, awakening people to living fellowship with God when they are made to live by the Spirit. This brings us to the third area for investigation.

THE SPIRIT AND ILLUMINATION

A word spoken but not heard does not profit us. In a sense, what we have said about the source of prophecy and Scripture in the Spirit stresses the objective side of revelation – the Spirit has spoken through individuals in space and in time.

But this is only part of the movement of the Spirit of God towards us in revelation. The word spoken must be 'heard'; that which is revealed must be 'seen'. Something must take place in us to complete the movement of God towards us in revelation, otherwise revelation 'hangs in the air' without fulfilling its goal of creating fellowship between God and man. This 'something' is the work of illumination which also is the Spirit's

work and is most clearly spoken of in 1 Corinthians 2:9–16, from which we quote:

> 'No eye has seen, no ear has heard, no mind has conceived what God has prepared for those who love him'– but God has revealed it to us by his Spirit. The Spirit searches all things, even the deep things of God. For who among men knows the thoughts of a man except the man's spirit within him? In the same way no-one knows the thoughts of God except the Spirit of God. We have not received the spirit of the world but the Spirit who is from God, that we may understand what God has freely given us.

Paul makes it clear in the words that follow that this revelatory work comes through the words that are given by the Spirit himself and spoken in the apostolic preaching. Although not accepted by the person without the Spirit, those who have the Spirit (spiritual men and women) accept them for what they are (vv.13–16).

It is evident, then, that the Spirit, who himself knows the fullness of God, invests himself in the words of the apostolic preaching in order through them to give himself to those who receive the word. Those who receive the word have their minds illuminated by the Spirit. This corresponds with what he has said elsewhere:

> I keep asking that the God of our Lord Jesus Christ, the glorious Father, may give you the Spirit of wisdom and revelation, so that you may know him better. I pray also that the eyes of your heart may be enlightened in order that you may know the hope to which he has called you, the riches of his glorious inheritance in the saints . . . (Eph. 1:17–18).

It makes sense to say that the Spirit who creates fellowship, the divine current of communication, the Go-Between God, should be involved at

TO THINK ABOUT . . .

**Are there differences, and if so what are they, between an
audience listening to someone proclaiming the Christian
gospel or expounding the Bible's message and an audience
listening to an enthusiast speaking about any other subject?**

both ends of the revelatory process. He is involved in the speaking and the hearing, the showing and the seeing. He enables revelation to both happen and be received. He is in the drawing near of God to people and of people to God. He crosses the divide between the two, and in such a way as to lead us to confess that all is of grace. He is able to reveal God because he himself is God. He is able to illuminate persons and interact with them because he himself is personal.

> **TO THINK ABOUT . . .**
>
> If this is true, are there any ways in which we may learn to hear what the Spirit is saying? How can we do this:
>
> a) individually?
> b) when we meet as the church?

With these things in mind, it now becomes essential to show how the Spirit who breathes through all creation and reveals God to humanity cannot be thought of without reference to Jesus Christ.

ASSIGNMENT 2

An Understanding of the Spirit in the New Testament

This assignment is designed to help you discover the way in which Luke, both in his Gospel and in the book of Acts, treats the theme of the Holy Spirit. It has often been said that Luke concentrates on dramatic action at the expense of other emphases.

You will need a good concordance to help you firstly trace all the references to the Spirit in the Gospel of Luke and Acts.

Then respond to these two tasks:

a. Gather and set down references in the Gospel and Acts to those occasions where Luke links the work of the Holy Spirit with dramatic action.

b. Discuss the view that the occurrence of dramatic events is not the only or even primary criterion for detecting the Spirit's action today. Give illustrations from your own life or that of your church where the Spirit's presence and action have been discerned either in dramatic action or in other ways. Use evidence from Luke/Acts to inform your answer.

The following New Testament references may also be helpful: Matthew 7:22–23; 1 Corinthians 12:1–3, 13:1–3; 1 John 4:1–6.

Write around 750 words.

UNIT 4

The Spirit as the Giver of Jesus

WE HAVE TAKEN NOTE of the role of the Spirit in imparting revelation. It is crucial to add that the supreme revelation of God is given in the person of Jesus Christ. That is why Christ is recognised as the Word of God who was with God in the beginning, who became a human being and who makes the God, whom no-one has ever seen, known in visible form (John 1:1, 14, 18). Properly speaking, the revelation which is the content of Scripture is Jesus Christ. He is the Word of God who is contained in Scripture and which was made flesh as Jesus of Nazareth. He is God speaking to humankind.

Once more, however, we must recognise the relationship between the Word which is spoken and the breath by which it is spoken. As in Hebrew the word *ruach* means breath, spirit or wind, so in Greek the word *pneuma* can mean breath, spirit or wind. As the creative word of God is uttered by the Spirit, so the revelatory and redemptive Word which is Jesus Christ is spoken or impelled into human history by the Spirit of God.

Once more we come to a crucial point which expands our understanding of the Spirit. Our inclination is to think of the Spirit as having been sent into the world by Christ. This is true. It may, however, obscure for us the equally important truth that the Son of God has come into the world through the Holy Spirit. The Spirit has given us Christ before Christ has given us the Spirit.

In this unit we trace this theme. Our concern is to show that it is by the Holy Spirit that the Word has become incarnate; it is by that same Spirit that the particular human identity of Jesus of Nazareth has become the bearer of the eternal Son of God. In support of this claim we notice in the biblical account of Christ the following aspects of the Holy Spirit's work.

PREPARING THE WAY FOR THE COMING OF IMMANUEL

That the Spirit opens up the way for the coming of Jesus is particularly noticeable in the Gospel of Luke. Suddenly, after years of God's apparent silence and the absence of prophecy, a flurry of spiritual activity breaks out. It begins with the promise of a son to Zechariah and Elizabeth. It is as if the barren years are past and the days of fulfilment have arrived. The son to be born 'will be filled with the Holy Spirit even from birth' (1:15).

Shortly afterwards the angel-messenger appears to Mary and she receives the promise that the Holy Spirit will come on her (1:35). When Elizabeth meets Mary, Elizabeth is filled with the Holy Spirit and pronounces a blessing on her (1:41).

When Elizabeth heard Mary's greeting, the baby leaped in her womb, and Elizabeth was filled with the Holy Spirit.

> **TO THINK ABOUT . . .**
> How do you think Elizabeth and Zechariah and Mary and Joseph must have felt as the Spirit of God laid these various privileges and responsibilities on them? How do you think you would have felt?

Mary herself, in an experience reminiscent of ecstasy in the Old Testament, is inspired to utter a psalm of praise to God as her spirit rejoices in God her Saviour (1:46–55). A similar experience engulfs Zechariah when John is born:

> His father Zechariah was filled with the Holy Spirit and prophesied (1:67).

Amongst other things he prophesies that his son will be a prophet of the Most High (1:76). John himself is said to grow 'and become strong in the Spirit' (1:80).

After the birth of Jesus, his parents are blessed by a righteous and devout man, Simeon. It is recorded that:

> the Holy Spirit was upon him. It had been revealed to him by the Holy Spirit that he would not die before he had seen the Lord's Christ (2:25, 26).

This revelation was fulfilled when:

> moved by the Spirit, he went into the temple courts.

Here he encountered Mary and Joseph and their child and blessed them with inspired words (2:26–32).

These brief pictures create an impression of a devout group of Jewish believers being prepared by the Spirit to receive the Messiah for whom they had hoped. Jesus is born into a circle of people who represent the best of Jewish devotion and in whom the fire of Old Testament faith is kept burning.

> ### TO THINK ABOUT . . .
> **Can you think of examples where you and other Christians have looked forward to and prayed for the fulfilling of God's promises, but when he has brought those promises to reality you were confused, cautious, unbelieving and unprepared?**

It is not that the Holy Spirit has been absent and then returns, but that in such a remnant as this the work of the Spirit is very much a living reality. God does not abandon his world, but even as it resists him he prepares it to receive the one who will redeem it.

Here we have the Spirit preparing the way for the coming of Immanuel, God with us, to comfort and redeem his people (Matt. 1:22–23). The one who had inspired the prophet to speak of his coming (Isa. 7:14) watches over his word to bring it to fulfilment (Jer. 1:12).

> ### TO THINK ABOUT . . .
> **What unfulfilled aspects of God's purposes for this world do *you* most long to see the Holy Spirit accomplish? Why do you answer in this way?**

ENTRUSTING THE SON OF GOD TO THE WOMB OF MARY

Jesus was conceived in Mary's womb through the action of the Spirit. She is told, as we have noted:

> The Holy Spirit will come upon you, and the power of the Most High will overshadow you. So the holy one to be born will be called the Son of God (Luke 1:35).

This promise was given while Mary was yet 'a virgin pledged to be married to a man named Joseph' (Luke 1:27). It happened therefore that:

> before they came together she was found to be with child through the Holy Spirit (Matt. 1:18);

and Joseph is told in a dream:

> what is conceived in her is from the Holy Spirit. She will give birth to a son, and you are to give him the name Jesus, because he will save his people from their sins (Matt. 1:20–21).

It is through the Spirit that the Son of God becomes incarnate in the womb of a virgin.

TO THINK ABOUT . . .

How does this statement leave you feeling about the role of women in the accomplishing of God's purposes?

This 'virgin birth' or (more accurately) 'virginal conception' is a sign of the action of God through the man Jesus. The creative Spirit, who overshadowed the waters at the birth of creation, here overshadows a young Jewish girl to perform in her womb a gracious, creative miracle. It is a miracle of new creation. The one to be born is given in order to renew a fallen race and to recreate the purpose of God. Into the old world is born the agent of the new world, and the Spirit who was present at the birth of the old is present at the birth of the new in the midst of the old.

Moreover, he is the active power that brings both to pass. Jesus Christ is not the product of the human race, not even of the most devout Jewish members of it. He is the result of the recreative power of God, working sovereignly within humanity by his Spirit to bring to birth a new people.

TO THINK ABOUT . . .

Why does the issue of the 'virgin birth' or 'virgin conception' raise such strong feelings? Why is defending it considered by many Christians to be of fundamental importance?

EMPOWERING THE LIFE AND MINISTRY OF JESUS CHRIST

Jesus was born of the Spirit in order to live in the Spirit. We find therefore that:

> the child grew and became strong; he was filled with wisdom, and the grace of God was upon him (Luke 2:40; cf. Isa. 11:1–3).

At the age of twelve he amazes the teachers in the temple with his understanding (Luke 2:46 –47, see also v.52). This is a sign of the Spirit resting upon him. It is, however, with his baptism that Jesus enters into the fullness of his mission. This baptism is recorded in all four Gospels as the time when:

> heaven was opened and the Holy Spirit descended on him in bodily form like a dove (Luke 3:22; cf. Matt. 3:16–17, Mark 1:10).

In the Gospel of John this occasion is the moment when John the Baptist recognises the fulfilment of a revelation given to him by God:

> The man on whom you see the Spirit come down and remain is he who will baptise with the Holy Spirit (John 1:33).

This verse expresses more fully the crucial role of Jesus. The Spirit descends on Jesus at his baptism, not because he was previously absent but to anoint Jesus for the ministry into which he now enters. Jesus is to be the one who baptises in the Holy Spirit, through whom the Spirit is mediated to bring the age of salvation and new life to sinners.

After his baptism the Spirit remains on Jesus and enables him to fulfil the mission for which he has been sent into the world. Jesus, full of the Spirit, is led by the Spirit to be tested in the wilderness (Luke 4:1).

> **TO THINK ABOUT . . .**
>
> **In the Bible the Spirit is constantly associated with mission to the world in all its need.**
>
> **In what ways does being a Christian, indwelt by the Holy Spirit, alter your attitude to the world, your concern to be informed about it, and your action in it?**

According to the picture presented by the Gospels, Jesus now exhibits a profound consciousness of the Spirit of God. He hears the Holy

> **TO THINK ABOUT . . .**
> **Is it significant for the Christian facing testing and temptation today that the Holy Spirit came on Jesus before his experience in the wilderness?**

Having proved more than equal to the test, he returns from the wilderness in the power of the Spirit (Luke 4:14) and proclaims his new awareness of his mission in the synagogue at Nazareth:

The Spirit of the Lord is on me, because he has anointed me to preach good news to the poor . . . to proclaim the year of the Lord's favour (Luke 4:18–19; cf. Isa. 61:1–2).

Spirit speaking in the Old Testament Scriptures (Matt. 22:43), understands his mighty acts of power as being accomplished by the Spirit of God (Matt. 12:28), and accuses those who denigrate his works of blaspheming against the Holy Spirit (Matt. 12:31; Luke 12:10). He speaks to the disciples of the willingness of the Father to give the Holy Spirit to those who ask (Luke 11:13), assures them of the fact that the Holy

Spirit will help them when they are on trial (Luke 12:12), and commands them to baptise in the name of Father, Son and Spirit (Matt. 28:19).

A fascinating glimpse is given into the inner life of Jesus in Luke 10:21 when we read:

> At that time Jesus, full of joy through the Holy Spirit, said, 'I praise you, Father, Lord of heaven and earth . . .'

Here we see the Spirit as the one who causes joy to well up in the heart of Jesus, overflowing in thanksgiving and praise and expressing the intimacy of the relationship of the Son with the Father who is Lord of heaven and earth (see also vv.22–24).

It is clear, then, that we are unable to understand either the life or the mission of Jesus other than as absolutely dependent on the Spirit. The Spirit of God is the activating power within Jesus, as was later recalled by Peter:

> You know what has happened throughout Judea, beginning in Galilee after the baptism that John preached – how God anointed Jesus of Nazareth with the Holy Spirit and power, and how he went around doing good and healing all who were under the power of the devil, because God was with him (Acts 10:37–8).

TO THINK ABOUT . . .
How does thinking of Jesus as dependent on the Spirit help you understand his true humanity? How does this help you understand your own relationship to God?

ENABLING THE SACRIFICIAL SELF-OFFERING OF JESUS

We have already drawn attention to the words in John 1:33 which point to Jesus as the one who both receives and imparts the Holy Spirit. Christ is the one who will baptise with the Holy Spirit.

It is significant that these words occur immediately after John the Baptist's reference to Jesus as the one who is 'the Lamb of God, who takes away the sin of the world' (1:29). The link is important. It is by taking away the sin of the world that Christ can mediate the Holy Spirit to those who believe.

Even here, in the self-offering of Jesus, the work of the Holy Spirit is to be recognised, although it is explicitly spoken of on only one occasion in the New Testament. That occasion is Hebrews 9:14:

> How much more, then, will the blood of Christ, who through the eternal Spirit offered himself unblemished to God, cleanse our consciences from acts that lead to death, so that we may serve the living God!

TO THINK ABOUT . . .
In what areas of sacrificial service and living are you most conscious that you cannot achieve anything effective without the enabling of the Spirit?

These words will recall the Servant of the Lord spoken of in Isaiah 42:1:

> I will put my Spirit on him and he will bring justice to the nations.

This is the Servant who is then portrayed in Isaiah 53 as he who 'poured out his soul unto death' (v.12). As the Spirit enabled the self-sacrifice spoken of in Isaiah 53, so in Hebrews 9:14 it is the eternal Spirit who enabled Jesus to offer himself as both priest and victim to cleanse his people. The Spirit is the motivating and enabling power behind the self-offering of Jesus throughout his life and then supremely in his death.

It is difficult to penetrate beyond this point and to ask what the Holy Spirit was doing when the Son of God gave himself over to death and for our sakes experienced abandonment by God at the cross. The New Testament itself says nothing, but perhaps it may validly be claimed that, as the Son of God journeyed into the darkness of death, he was accompanied on his way by the Holy Spirit who therefore was able to be the agent of the next moment in the earthly existence of the Son of God.

THE RESURRECTION OF JESUS BY THE SPIRIT OF HOLINESS

According to Romans 1:4, Christ

> through the Spirit of holiness was declared with power to be the Son of God, by his resurrection from the dead.

The Spirit was the active power behind the raising of Jesus. With even greater clarity, 1 Peter 3:18 asserts:

> He was put to death in the body but made alive by the Spirit.

If it is correct to understand the Spirit as accompanying the Son of God on his journey into the abandonment of death, it is by that same Spirit that the Son is retrieved from death and raised to new life. We may see in this the fulfilment of the words quoted by Peter on the day of Pentecost:

> You will not abandon me to the grave, nor will you let your Holy One see decay. You have made known to me the paths of life; you will fill me with joy in your presence (Acts 2:27–8; cf. Psa. 16:8–11).

It is by the Spirit that Christ is preserved from corruption and restored to new life.

> **TO THINK ABOUT . . .**
> Consider the assurance that the power of God's Spirit which raised Jesus from the dead is at work in Christians. How might a Christian expect that power to be seen in his or her life and in the face of death?

SUMMARY

By now it should be clear that Jesus Christ has indeed come to us by the Holy Spirit. The Spirit prepared the way for his coming, caused him to be conceived in Mary's womb, enabled and empowered his ministry, was the means of his sacrificial self-offering at the cross and restored him to a new dimension of life by the resurrection. Jesus Christ is the supreme gift of God by the Holy Spirit to this world.

This is not to say that Jesus was merely the most Spirit-filled man who has ever lived. He was that, but more besides. It was through the Spirit that the eternal Son of God was joined to a distinct and individual human personality. Through the Spirit, human nature was rendered capable of bearing in incarnation the eternal Son of God, in such a way as to present us with the one human person, Jesus of Nazareth, who is fully God and fully man. For this inexpressible gift, we are eternally grateful to the Spirit of God.

UNIT 5

The Spirit as the Gift of Jesus

NOW WE TURN THE TABLES. The Spirit is the giver of Jesus and is also the gift of Jesus. Jesus comes to us by the Spirit and the Spirit comes to us by Jesus. This is what is indicated in John 1:33:

The man on whom you see the Spirit come down and remain is he who will baptise with the Holy Spirit.

It is now our task to explore this theme.

THE SPIRIT – THE GIFT OF JESUS TO HIS CHURCH

In Acts 2:33 the apostle Peter declares:

Exalted to the right hand of God, he has received from the Father the promised Holy Spirit and has poured out what you now see and hear.

The dramatic events of the Day of Pentecost recorded in Acts 2:1–13 are understood as the 'outpouring' or baptism of the Spirit by Christ upon the Church. The Spirit comes as the mighty wind (v.2) and with tongues of fire (v.3) to fill the waiting believers.

> **TO THINK ABOUT . . .**
> In what ways are the pictures of fire and wind helpful for expressing the work of the Holy Spirit?

The incident is strangely reminiscent of the activity of the Spirit in the Old Testament, as the Spirit overwhelms the disciples and causes them to speak in other tongues (v.4), to behave like drunken men (v.13) and to testify with great boldness to Jesus Christ (v.11, vv.14ff). Compare this with the experiences of Saul in 1 Samuel 10:5–7, 9–11.

Acts 2:11 '. . . we hear them declaring the wonders of God in our own tongues.'

> **TO THINK ABOUT . . .**
> What similarities are there between Pentecost and the experiences of Saul? What was really happening on these occasions? How would you have felt if you had been there?

It is important to note that this incident is interpreted by Peter as the gift of the promised Spirit from the ascended Christ. It may be seen, therefore, as the initial fulfilment of John 1:33: 'He . . . will baptise with the Holy Spirit' (see also Acts 1:4–5). It is clearly implied in Acts 2:33 that now the Christ is exalted he is in a position to fulfil the promise of the Old Testament and of his own ministry by pouring out the Spirit.

This link between the gift of the Spirit and the work of Christ is also indicated in John 7:37–39:

> 'If anyone is thirsty, let him come to me and drink. Whoever believes in me, as the Scripture has said, streams of living water will flow from within him.' By this he meant the Spirit, whom those who believed in him were later to receive. Up to that time the Spirit had not been given, since Jesus had not yet been glorified.

According to the Gospel of John, the lifting up of Jesus on the cross, his resurrection and ascension are to be understood as the glorifying of Jesus (John 17:1–5). Through cross and resurrection, the glory of Jesus is revealed. The clear implication is that, before the Spirit can be given as the permanent and abiding presence of God within his people, the work of Christ as the sacrificial Lamb of God must be fulfilled. He must die, rise and ascend, completing his earthly ministry and opening up the way to the Father for those who believe, so that the life of God may be poured upon them in the Spirit. Once this reconciling work is accomplished, the Spirit who has been promised may be given.

TO THINK ABOUT . . .
The Spirit cannot be given until after the work of Christ as the sacrificial Lamb of God has been fulfilled. Does this say anything about the experience of God's Spirit in *our* lives?

Christ as God incarnate becomes the mediator of the Spirit to those who are his. This does not imply that the Spirit is absent from the world. We have already seen that the Spirit is the active presence of God within the created sphere. But it does imply that, because of Christ's reconciling work, there is a new mode of the Spirit's presence. He is present not just as Creator-Spirit but as Redeemer-Spirit, indwelling those who believe and opening up an abiding fellowship with the Father through the Son. This new mode of the Spirit's presence is indicated in John 14:17 where Jesus says:

> 'The world cannot accept him, because it neither sees him nor knows him. But you know him, for he lives with you and will be in you.'

As the gift of Jesus, therefore, the Spirit opens up a new world for those who are Christ's.

TO THINK ABOUT . . .
How would you describe to a non-Christian what blessings the Spirit has opened up for you in this abiding fellowship with the Father through the Son?

It is with this new world that much of the rest of this study manual is concerned, and the following point is crucial for our understanding of this new world.

THE SPIRIT – THE CONTINUING PRESENCE OF JESUS CHRIST IN THE WORLD

The Spirit is now the continuation of the presence of Christ without limitations of space or time. This is what Jesus taught his disciples. He first of all tells them:

> I will ask the Father, and he will give you another Counsellor to be with you for ever – the Spirit of truth (John 14:16–17).

and later adds:

> But I tell you the truth: It is for your good that I am going away. Unless I go away, the Counsellor will not come to you; but if I go, I will send him to you (John 16:7).

These are highly significant words for understanding the Spirit and his present work. Jesus teaches:

THE SPIRIT IS 'ANOTHER COUNSELLOR'

The word here translated 'Counsellor' is more literally translated as 'Paraclete' and carries the meanings 'Encourager', 'Comforter' and 'Advocate'. The word 'Counsellor' is used in the Revised Standard and New International Versions to hold all these meanings together.

Just as Jesus has been with his disciples, encouraging and guiding them and interpreting to them his teaching, so when he is gone they will not be left as orphans. The Spirit of truth will lead them into truth (John 16:13), he will support and encourage them, he will be with them as an advocate when they are put on trial (Matt. 10:19–20, Mark 13:11). Literally 'Paraclete' refers to one who is 'called alongside' to help.

In 1 John 2:1 the same word is used of the ascended Christ who represents us to the Father. This highlights the fact that the Holy Spirit is *another* Counsellor. The word implies that he is another of the same kind as Jesus himself. Indeed, the Holy Spirit is the one through whom Christ continues to be present with his own. This is why in John 14:18 Jesus can say:

> I will not leave you as orphans; I will come to you.

The Spirit is Christ himself, present in a different form. There is an identity between Christ and the Spirit and at the same time a difference.

TO THINK ABOUT . . .

Does this idea of the Spirit as the continuing presence of Jesus Christ in the world leave you feeling:

helped?	challenged?
encouraged?	some other reaction?
baffled?	

Here once more we have the mystery of the Holy Trinity, the unity in distinction in God. This identity of the Risen Lord and the Spirit is referred to by the apostle Paul, when he says:

> Now the Lord is the Spirit, and where the Spirit of the Lord is there is freedom (2 Cor. 3:17).

This helps us to understand the second point about the teaching of Jesus:

THE SPIRIT'S COMING IS FOR OUR GOOD

The presence of Jesus through the Spirit is to our advantage.

> It is for your good that I am going away. Unless I go away, the Counsellor will not come to you (John 16:7).

Here the going away refers to the journey to the cross and to death, and beyond that to the Father. By this going away, Jesus makes possible the coming of the Spirit. His coming is for the disciples' good, precisely because the presence of Christ with his people is no longer limited in space and time by the conditions of the incarnation but is made universal by the Spirit. Christ can promise always to be with the disciples (Matt. 28:20) because by the Spirit his personal presence is made universally real. The Lord is the Spirit. The disciples of Christ have therefore an incredible advantage, the abiding and continuing presence of the Lord in every situation and circumstance.

'It is for your good that I am going away. Unless I go away, the Counsellor will not come to you' (John 16:7).

TO THINK ABOUT . . .

How would you have reacted to the words of Jesus?

In what ways do we grow in faith and Christian maturity when our own hopes and dreams are dashed, only to be replaced by something better?

We come now to a third point:

THE SPIRIT'S PRESENCE IS PERMANENT

The Spirit is with God's people for ever.

> I will ask the Father and he will give you another Counsellor to be with you for ever (John 14:16).

The presence of the Spirit, as the one in whom Christ abides with his people, is to be permanent.

Here we have a major and important difference between the work of the Holy Spirit in the Old and New Testaments. In the Old Testament the Spirit came on individuals for specific tasks and functions and then departed. In the New Testament the Church knows the Spirit as a perma-nent, indwelling reality. He does not depart from them. There may be times when the Spirit equips for particular tasks (as we shall see), but he also resides permanently and continually in the Church and makes Christ present forever in and among his people.

It is for this reason that the Spirit is the gift of Christ to his Church. He bestows upon God's people permanent fellowship with the Father in the Son.

TO THINK ABOUT . . .

Reflect on the term 'the gift of the Holy Spirit'. What does the fact that the Spirit comes as a gift tell us about how we are to live the Christian life?

THE SPIRIT WORKS TO GLORIFY JESUS CHRIST

The Holy Spirit is at work in the Church, bringing its members into a full realisation of that which has been done for them and given to them in Jesus Christ. This is shown by the words of Jesus:

> He will bring glory to me by taking from what is mine and making it known to you. All that belongs to the Father is mine. That is why I said the Spirit will take from what is mine and make it known to you (John 16:14–15).

CHRIST IS GOD'S LAST WORD

The Spirit is not be understood as superceding Christ, so that in the age of the Spirit Jesus Christ is no longer necessary or of interest. Because Christ is the Son of God it is impossible to supercede him. In him all the fullness of God was pleased to dwell and the fullness of our life is in him (Col. 1:9–10). Christ is God's last Word and after him there comes no other word (Heb. 1:1–4).

The work of the Spirit, therefore, is not to surpass Christ but to take us into the fullness of Christ, to enable us to see and experience that the eternal God is here for us in Christ and that we will never exhaust him. The Spirit draws our attention to Christ, he focuses on him, he causes us to see again and again that 'in him was life and that life was the light of men' (John 1:4).

THE FLOODLIGHT MINISTRY

This aspect of the Spirit's work has been aptly called 'the floodlight ministry'. J.I. Packer has expressed it as follows:

> When floodlighting is well done, the floodlights are so placed that you do not see them; you are not in fact supposed to see where the light is coming from; what you are meant to see is just the building on which the floodlights are trained. The intended effect is to make it visible when otherwise it would not be seen for the darkness, and to maximise its dignity by throwing all its details into relief so that you see it properly. This perfectly illustrates the Spirit's new covenantal role. He is, so to speak, the hidden floodlight shining on the Saviour. . . . The Spirit, we might say, is the matchmaker, the celestial marriage broker, whose role is to bring us and Christ together and ensure that we stay together. As the second Paraclete, the Spirit leads us constantly to the original Paraclete, who himself draws near . . . through the second Paraclete's coming to us.

TO THINK ABOUT . . .
Do you find this image of 'the floodlight' a helpful way of describing the Spirit's ministry? If so, how does it help you and how would you use it to explain to someone else the role of the Holy Spirit in relation to Jesus?

By permission of the BBC.

The floodlight ministry is not the whole of the Spirit's work. We have already seen many other dimensions. But it is *the central facet* of his work and is consistent with all that we have so far covered. If the Spirit is the breath that enables the creative and redemptive Word to be uttered, then it is that same Word that he speaks into the lives of individuals. This is how the Spirit's work is to be recognised. Any spirit (teaching, ideology, truth claim, religious experience, etc) that does not point to Christ, is inconsistent with him or claims to go beyond him to some other fountainhead, is not the Holy Spirit.

This is how you can recognise the Spirit of God: Every spirit that acknowledges that Jesus Christ has come in the flesh is from God, but every spirit that does not acknowledge that Jesus Christ has come in the flesh is not from God (1 John 4:2).

> ### TO THINK ABOUT . . .
> **In the light of the above, how can you recognise the Spirit of God at work?**
>
> **Are there other, sinister, sources of spiritual power in the depth of the human soul or in the world at large? What are they and how do we recognise the Spirit in distinction from them?**

In exploring the theme of the Spirit as the gift of Jesus, we have attempted to understand the relationship between the exalted Christ and the outpoured Spirit. Through the Spirit Christ is personally present with his people. The Spirit leads the Church into that life which is ours in Christ, drawing our attention to him. He prompts the confession that 'Jesus Christ is Lord' (1 Cor. 12:3).

We will now go on to explore how the Spirit fulfils his work in the Church as a community and in the individuals who are its members.

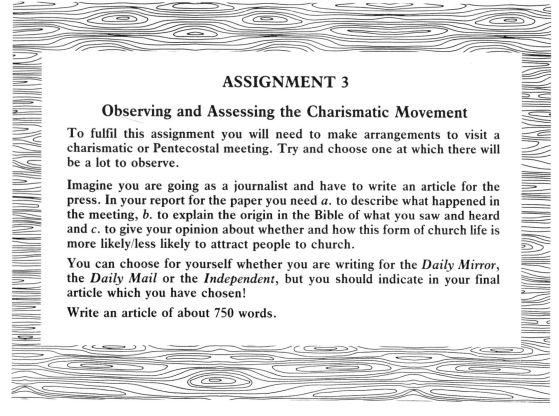

ASSIGNMENT 3

Observing and Assessing the Charismatic Movement

To fulfil this assignment you will need to make arrangements to visit a charismatic or Pentecostal meeting. Try and choose one at which there will be a lot to observe.

Imagine you are going as a journalist and have to write an article for the press. In your report for the paper you need *a.* to describe what happened in the meeting, *b.* to explain the origin in the Bible of what you saw and heard and *c.* to give your opinion about whether and how this form of church life is more likely/less likely to attract people to church.

You can choose for yourself whether you are writing for the *Daily Mirror*, the *Daily Mail* or the *Independent*, but you should indicate in your final article which you have chosen!

Write an article of about 750 words.

UNIT 6

The Spirit and the Church

THE CHURCH OF JESUS CHRIST is the community of the Holy Spirit. The Church came into being as a direct consequence of the coming of the Holy Spirit and continues to exist in him. Without the Spirit the Church ceases to be the Church. Without the Spirit the Church cannot do the work of God effectively. The dependence of the people of God on the Spirit of God is total.

It is not that the Spirit is the exclusive possession of an élite within the Church, neither is it that the Spirit is an 'optional extra', about whom the majority of good Christians need not bother. The Spirit of God is absolutely essential for the very life of the people of God. These are big claims! It is necessary, therefore, to justify them from the New Testament.

TO THINK ABOUT . . .

In what ways can people treat the Spirit as an optional extra?

Why is it often difficult for Christians to recognise their total dependence on the Spirit of God?

THE SPIRIT AND THE GATHERING OF THE CHURCH

The Church as we know it came into being on the day of Pentecost, when the disciples of Jesus were together and it is recorded:

> Suddenly a sound like the blowing of a violent wind came from heaven and filled the whole house where they were sitting. They saw what seemed to be tongues of fire that separated and came to rest on each of them. All of them were filled with the Holy Spirit and began to speak in other tongues as the Holy Spirit enabled them (Acts 2:2–4).

PARALLELS WITH THE OT

The passage above describes the coming of the Spirit, bringing the Church into being. In it there are some significant parallels with the Old Testament. The idea of the Spirit as the wind is clearly rooted in the Old Testament. The kind of experience the apostles enter into is reminiscent of the way the Spirit came upon the seventy elders in Numbers 11:24–27 and upon Saul in 1 Samuel 10:5–13.

When the Spirit comes he enables the apostles to declare the deeds of God in other languages, and people from 'every nation under heaven' are able to hear the wonders of God in their own languages (Acts 2:5–12).

PENTECOST REVERSES THE EXPERIENCE AT BABEL

When this passage in Acts is contrasted with the story of the Tower of Babel in Genesis 11:1–9, we begin to understand the meaning of Pentecost. At the Tower of Babel the judgement of God led to the division of the people of God into language groups, dividing and separating them. On the Day of Pentecost the precise opposite happens. Divided and broken humanity begins to come together. Because of the Spirit of God a new people is formed, drawn from every nation under the sun and speaking a common language because of the Spirit of God.

TO THINK ABOUT . . .

What are some problems in personal and international relationships which are caused by language barriers?

What does it mean that the people of God speak a common language because of the Spirit?

The Spirit of God initiates the Church. He brings it into being and is the means of its coming to birth. The Church is therefore the community of the Spirit. Without the Spirit the Church would not and could not exist as the new, restored people of God.

TO THINK ABOUT . . .

How do the events at Pentecost shape our understanding of the Spirit's ongoing work in the Church?

THE SPIRIT AND THE NATURE OF THE CHURCH

The dependence of the Church on the Spirit is illustrated in two particular images of the Church which are used in the New Testament.

THE CHURCH AS THE BODY OF CHRIST

'There is one body and one Spirit' (Eph. 4:4). The image of the Church as the Body of Christ is particularly found in Ephesians 4:1–16, Romans 12:5 and 1 Corinthians 12:12–31. It is a very important image, suggesting the variety-in-unity of the Church and the pre-eminent role of Christ as the Head of the Body (Eph. 4:15, Col. 1:18). The Spirit is the breath that gives life to the Body, enabling it to live, move and work. Christians are related to each other and to the Head as parts of the Body and are animated by the Spirit of Christ. He is the living breath who moves us.

> For we were all baptised by one Spirit into one body . . . (1 Cor. 12:13).

TO THINK ABOUT . . .

We often apply the image of the body only to life in a local church. But what relationships should we expect the Holy Spirit to create between local congregations and the wider fellowship of believers, between churches and the Church?

THE CHURCH AS THE TEMPLE OF THE SPIRIT

A second important image is that of the Church as the Temple of God. 1 Corinthians 3:16 makes this particularly clear:

> Don't you know that you yourselves are God's temple and that God's Spirit lives in you?

The Old Testament temple was the dwelling place of God, the place where his glory was made known (Ezek. 10:4, Hagg. 2:9). In Jesus Christ the Temple of God was a living person of whom it could be said:

> The Word became flesh and made his dwelling among us. We have seen his glory, the glory of the One and Only, who came from the Father . . .

After the ascension it is the Church which is the Temple in which the Spirit lives. The location of God's dwelling with humankind was moved from being a building, to being a person, to being a community. The Father and the Son have made their dwelling in the Church by the Holy Spirit.

All of this is, of course, a prelude to the day which is the hope of all creation, the day when the whole of creation becomes the dwelling place, the temple, of God. This is the day anticipated in the Book of Revelation:

> And I heard a loud voice from the throne saying, 'now the dwelling of God is with men, and he will live with them. They will be his people, and God himself will be with them and be their God. He will wipe every tear from their eyes. There will be no more death or mourning or crying or pain, for the old order of things has passed away' (21:3–4).

The contemplation of the day when God will be 'all in all' (1 Cor. 15:28) brings us to our next point.

TO THINK ABOUT . . .

A temple is holy, to be used for no other purpose than the service of God. How are Christians to behave as befits the temple, yet live in the world?

THE SPIRIT, THE CHURCH AND THE AGE OF FULFILMENT

THE SPIRIT OF THE END-TIME

The coming of the Spirit on the Day of Pentecost was more than the outpouring of spiritual power upon the early believers. It was the beginning of a new age. It was the dawn of the age of fulfilment.

This is the meaning of the prophecy of Joel, which is quoted by Peter in explanation of the meaning of Pentecost. It begins:

> In the last days, God says, I will pour out my Spirit on all people' (see Acts 2:17–21).

Peter then goes on to speak of the activity of the Spirit in God's people and connects this with the upheavals that are to take place in the world 'before the coming of the great and glorious day of the Lord' (v.20). The point is that the coming of the Spirit at Pentecost is part of the eschatological (ie. end-time) fulfilment of Old Testament prophecies concerning the world's final liberation.

This day of fulfilment had already begun in the ministry of Jesus, as is frequently indicated in the Gospels (eg. Luke 1:46–55, 11:20). It was for the fulfilment of this Old Testament expectation that the Spirit of the Lord was poured out upon Jesus (Luke 3:21–22, 4:18–19).

TO THINK ABOUT . . .

Read Luke 4:18–19. Pause over these images and descriptions of Jesus' ministry.

In what ways today do you see the Spirit at work, bringing good news to the poor, proclaiming freedom for prisoners, giving sight to the blind and releasing the oppressed?

When Jesus was anointed at his baptism, it was not because he previously lacked the Holy Spirit. If John the Baptist was filled with the Spirit from his birth (Luke 1:15), how much more was Jesus! Rather, when Jesus was anointed with the Spirit at his baptism, a new age dawns, the age of fulfilment and liberation, and Jesus is equipped by the Spirit to be the one through whom that age might break into the world of human beings, liberating them from the oppressions of evil and of the evil one. This is what immediately begins to happen (see Luke 4:31ff).

Luke 4:31–36. In the synagogue there was a man possessed by . . . an evil spirit . . . 'Be quiet!' Jesus said sternly. 'Come out of him! . . . All the people were amazed and said to each other, . . . 'With authority and power he gives orders to evil spirits and they come out!'

Understanding this enables us to grasp what happened for the Church at the day of Pentecost. At that time, and on the basis of what Christ achieved in death and resurrection, the Spirit comes on the Church, bringing the age of fulfilment upon those who believe. Empowered by the Spirit they become agents of this age of fulfilment. This brings us to a further point.

THE CHURCH OF THE END-TIME

The Church is the community of people who have already entered into the age of fulfilment. In other words, while continuing to be a part of the created order, outwardly indistinguishable from the rest of humanity, they have already entered into a dimension of God's life which means that the power of the transcendent God is transforming them.

This is what Hebrews 6:4–6 means when it refers to those who:

have been enlightened, who have tasted the heavenly gift, who have shared in the Holy Spirit,

who have tasted the goodness of the word of God and the powers of the coming age.

Similarly, Paul can refer to Christians as those:

on whom the fulfilment of the ages has come (1 Cor. 10:11).

and to the Holy Spirit as a present

deposit guaranteeing our inheritance until the redemption of those who are God's possession (Eph.1:14).

The future is already present in the Church. By the Spirit, the power of the age to come is present and manifest in the Church.

If we ask what the decisive difference is between the activity of the Spirit in the Old Testament and that in the New, the answer must be that what was known sporadically and occasionally in the Old becomes an abiding reality in the New. The Spirit was known in Israel in his equipping of particular *individuals* for particular tasks. In the Church he is known as the one who is poured out upon *all*, with the result that:

your sons and daughters will prophesy, your young men will see visions, your old men will dream dreams. Even on my servants, both men and women, I will pour out my Spirit in those days (Acts 2:17–18).

It is the universality and permanence of the Spirit's coming which characterises this age of fulfilment. It is indeed the age of the Spirit.

THE BAPTISM OF THE HOLY SPIRIT

At this point it is helpful to take our first look at a phrase much discussed in recent years, that of 'baptism in the Holy Spirit'. Once we understand that Pentecost marks the beginning of the age of the Spirit, we are in a position to understand the prophecy of John the Baptist recorded in each of the Gospels:

> I baptise you with water for repentance. But after me will come one who is more powerful than I, whose sandals I am not fit to carry. He will baptise you with the Holy Spirit and with fire (Matt. 3:11 cf. Mark 1:8, Luke 1:16, John 1:32–34).

These words are also found on the lips of Jesus with clear reference to the event of Pentecost (Acts 1:4–5).

TO THINK ABOUT . . .
How do you feel on hearing the phrase 'the baptism of the Holy Spirit':

confused?   grateful?
excited?   some other?
fearful?

What experiences have caused you to feel as you do?

The baptism of the Holy Spirit appears to convey the entirety of what comes to fulfilment in the Church because of Jesus Christ. To be baptised in the Spirit is to enter into this new reality of fulfilment with all the life-changing potential that this involves. This includes the outpouring of power on the Church and its members, but also comprises all the other aspects of the work of God in those who believe.

As the Church came into being through the coming of the Spirit on the day of Pentecost, so now individuals enter into the Church only when the Spirit comes to them and incorporates them into the Body of Christ, causing the age of fulfilment to dawn upon them. This is the meaning of 1 Corinthians 12:12–13 where Paul says:

> The body is a unit, though it is made up of many parts; and though all its parts are many, they form one body. So it is with Christ. For we were all baptised by one Spirit into one body – whether Jews or Greeks, slave or free – and we were all given one Spirit to drink.

We see here how appropriate it is that the Church should mark the entry of new members to the Body through the act of baptism. Baptism is rich in symbolism and amongst its meanings is that of being plunged into a new realm, the realm of the Spirit, just as a person is plunged into the waters of baptism. The Spirit is the hallmark of the Church and of the believer within the Church, so that Paul can say emphatically:

> And if anyone does not have the Spirit of Christ, he does not belong to Christ (Rom. 8:9).

What this means for the individual we shall consider more closely in the next unit, but first we consider what the baptism of the Spirit might mean for the Church as a community.

TO THINK ABOUT . . .
Before moving on, consider what you would expect to be the marks of a Spirit-baptised church and the evidences of the Spirit's presence.

THE CHURCH IN THE POWER OF THE HOLY SPIRIT

The coming of the Spirit on the Church is a powerful and mighty act of God. The Spirit of fellowship comes to create a dynamic and transforming fellowship with God and with others in Christ. This is precisely what we see in the early chapters of Acts as individuals repent, believe, are baptised and receive the Holy Spirit (2:38), and as a new community comes into being where a greater bond surpasses the old ties of culture, class, possessions and self-interest (Acts 2: 42–47).

In all this the Church is the expression of the age to come in the here and now. It lives by the power of the Spirit as surely as it came to be by the Spirit. In community terms, this may be seen in the following evidences of the Spirit's life.

THE CHURCH WORSHIPS BY THE SPIRIT

When in the early chapters of Acts the Spirit comes, one sign of this is that the worship of God comes readily to the people of God. In Acts 2:4 they are filled with the Spirit of God and begin to speak in other tongues. In Acts 2:11 this is interpreted to mean that they are 'declaring the wonders of God'. In Acts 2:42–47 they are said to be 'filled with awe' and to meet together every day in the temple courts praising God. When the Spirit falls upon the household of Cornelius, they too speak in tongues and praise God (10:46). There is an inescapable link between the Spirit and worship.

Paul sees one of the distinguishing marks of Christians is that they 'worship by the Spirit of God' (Phil. 3:3). The Spirit himself enables the Church to know and confess 'Abba, Father' in worship (Rom. 8:15). It is clear from the list of spiritual gifts in 1 Corinthians 12:7–11 that gatherings for worship were marked by the manifestation of the Spirit for the common good. Far from being dominated by one person, early Christian worship meetings were times of participation, when people with varying gifts could pray or speak for the good of all (1 Cor. 14:26 –33). It was the Spirit who enabled this participation. It was not unstructured worship but Spirit-led worship.

> **TO THINK ABOUT . . .**
>
> **Are you encouraged or disheartened by the ferment and changes in many churches today in patterns of worship?**
>
> **What strengths or weaknesses do you think such changes have?**

THE CHURCH SERVES BY THE SPIRIT

This is seen in the emphasis on spiritual gifts, the 'charismata' or 'gifts of grace' which have been bestowed on the Church and its members by the Spirit.

There are at least three lists of spiritual gifts given in the New Testament, and none of them is identical.

In **Romans 12:6–8** the list includes prophesying, serving, teaching, encouraging, contributing and leading, all necessary gifts in the community life of the Church.

In **Ephesians 4:7–13** the gifts of Christ are seen as people who exercise leadership functions within the Church: apostles, prophets, evangelists and pastor-teachers.

In **1 Corinthians 12:7–11** the gifts listed include the word of wisdom, the word of knowledge, faith, gifts of healing, miraculous powers, prophecy, discernment of spirits, speaking in tongues and interpretation of tongues. These appear from the context to be gifts that might particularly have found expression in early Christian gatherings.

It may be helpful to make a number of points about these gifts:

i. The lists cited appear to be *representative samples* of spiritual gifts rather than an exhaustive tally. No doubt there are as many other gifts as the Spirit determines there should be. Certainly the custom in some circles of referring to 'the nine gifts' (those in 1 Cor. 12) seems unnecessarily restrictive. It is perhaps more accurate to think in terms of the multi-faceted work of the Holy Spirit which can take many forms and find expression in varying spiritual gifts.

TO THINK ABOUT . . .
In what areas do you find it difficult to cope with the fact that the Spirit gifts and uses people in ways quite different from yourself? Why is it easier to want other people to be just like ourselves?

---

ii. It is *unhelpful to make too rigid definitions* of individual spiritual gifts. No doubt there is considerable overlap between, for instance, a word of knowledge (a revelation of an item of information) and a word of wisdom (a revelation of a wise course of action). Perhaps also the boundary between exhortation and prophecy is not very clear. Indeed, much of what is today called prophecy may better be understood as exhortation.

iii. It is helpful to understand *the spectrum of spiritual gifts.* The gifts already mentioned include:

- experiences which are highly intuitive (*eg.* speaking in tongues);
- abilities which are largely rational (*eg.* teaching, leading) and
- qualities which are partly circumstantial (*eg.* contributing – some people just have more money than others!).

'*Put the bill on my account, please.*'

TO THINK ABOUT . . .
What circumstances are you in and what assets do you have which the Spirit could use?

What Paul is really trying to stress is that whatever form the activity of the Spirit takes, it is a gift and not something to boast about. It would be a mistake to imagine that any gift is better than another because it is, say, more intuitive. Likewise, it would be wrong to devalue a gift because it is less rational than others (1 Thess. 5:19–22). All gifts have their place in the service of the Church and of God. Because the Spirit is Lord of all parts of our lives, whether our conscious reason, our unconscious intuition or our circumstances, we should expect him to work through all parts of our lives.

What determines whether a gift is really spiritual is not its unusual character but the purpose for which it is used and the effect it has. This is Paul's whole argument in 1 Corinthians 12, a chapter which will repay careful study. The Spirit manifests himself through the members of Christ's body for the common good of all, not for the private gratification of some (12:7, 24 –26). The spiritual value of a gift is to be measured according to whether it 'edifies' or 'builds up' God's people (1 Cor. 14:1–5).

TO THINK ABOUT . . .
Which gifts of the Spirit are especially suited to the needs and conditions of our age?

---

iv. Our *model for understanding* spiritual gifts is important. Often they have been thought of rather statically as individual gifts that individuals possess. We are then tempted to compare ourselves with one another and either feel proud or inferior as the case may be. It may be better to recognise that we do not *possess* any gift. We are, however, indwelt by the Spirit and the Spirit is able freely to manifest any gift through any Christian, according to the need of the situation.

This is sometimes called the 'situational' view of the gifts in contrast to the 'constituted' view. It offers a more dynamic way of thinking of the Spirit and his gifts, and stresses that our relationship to the Spirit of God is the crucial factor in our service of God. We none of us have anything that we did not receive from God.

TO THINK ABOUT . . .

Pause with this until you feel you understand the point being made.

Is this 'situational' view of spiritual gifts a helpful way of understanding how the Spirit works? How do you feel about never being sure how the Spirit will use you at any time or in any situation?

THE CHURCH FULFILS ITS MISSION BY THE SPIRIT

The Spirit is said by Jesus to 'go out from the Father' (John 15:26). We might describe him as the outgoing Spirit. Wherever the Spirit goes, there is a corresponding outgoing movement. When the Spirit came upon the early Church, the immediate response was an outgoing one. The apostles spoke the word of God boldly and effectively with the result that thousands were converted to Christ and joined the Church.

We see this pattern repeated in Acts 4. The Spirit came upon the Church again so that:

> they were all filled with the Holy Spirit and spoke the word of God boldly (4:31).

The book of Acts records the rapid growth of the early Church in the power of the Spirit.

TO THINK ABOUT . . .

In what ways is the Spirit thrusting your church into proclamation and service in the community?

Is it true that worship which is really in Spirit and in truth will inspire a church to look out and go out into the world in mission?

Church history repeats the lesson that people find life in God when the Spirit revives the Church and thrusts it into proclamation and service in the communities in which it is set. The Spirit empowers the Church for mission – joining in the outgoing movement of God into the world, seeking that people should be reconciled to God.

THE CHURCH IS GUIDED BY THE HOLY SPIRIT

In fulfilling its mission to the world, the Church of Christ (and individual churches within the whole Church) needs the guidance of the Spirit. The difficulties and challenges the Church faces are many and various. There are decisions to be made about how to serve the cause of Christ in the very different circumstances and cultures within which it is set. The Bible contains the fundamental truths of the faith, but it does not legislate for any and every circumstance or decision which we must make.

At this point we are relying on the wisdom that comes from continual reflection on God's Word and our ability to sense the mind of the Spirit. Because we are all fallible, discerning the mind of the Spirit on many issues is best done by the Church as a community. For this reason, Jesus told his disciples that they would not be left in the dark once he had left them:

> But when he, the Spirit of truth, comes, he will guide you into all truth (John 16:13).

We see this promise being fulfilled in Acts:

- in 11:28 we find the prophet Agabus predicting through the Spirit a severe famine, enabling the Church to take action;
- in 13:2 the church at Antioch is directed by the Spirit to set aside Barnabas and Saul for mission work;
- in 15:28 the Church is guided by the Spirit over a highly divisive issue at the Council of Jerusalem and is able to say: 'It seemed good to the Holy Spirit and to us . . .';
- in 16:6 we hear of Paul being 'kept by the Holy Spirit from preaching the word in the province of Asia' and in the following verse indicates that when they tried to enter Bithynia 'the Spirit of Jesus would not allow them to';

- in 20:22 Paul speaks of being 'compelled by the Spirit' to go to Jerusalem.

The Church exists under the Lordship of Christ in the Spirit and therefore is assured of the guiding presence of the Spirit in its mission.

TO THINK ABOUT . . .

If church meetings are to be times when the church opens itself to the guidance of the Holy Spirit, what form should such meetings take? How should they and how should they not be conducted?

IN SUMMARY

We have noted in this unit that the Church in the New Testament is the community of the Holy Spirit. It has its origin and its life in the Spirit of God. Where this ceases to be the case, the Church no longer exists in its true form but has become a society of religious people. So this unit has direct relevance to the way the Church is now. To recover the sense of being a community which lives, works, worships, proclaims and serves in the power of the Spirit is a crucial challenge for today.

UNIT 7

The Spirit and the Believer

THE GROUND WE HAVE SO FAR COVERED enables us to approach the subject of the Spirit and the individual believer. Often when the Spirit is thought about, the individual's experience immediately comes to mind. This manual has sought to avoid this by looking first to the wider works of the Spirit in creation and redemption, and then examining the Spirit's work in the Christian community. Now we are in a position to see, in the light of all that has been said, what the Spirit does in individual believers.

TO THINK ABOUT . . .

Pause to note down the ways in which the Spirit has been at work in your life. At the end of the unit see if you want to extend the list.

What have been significant growth points for you and how have you recognised the Spirit at work?

In Unit 4 we considered the work of the Spirit as the Giver of Jesus and traced the ways in which the humanity of Jesus was the result of the Spirit's activity. In the Church, the Spirit is concerned to produce a community of people made in the image of Christ. In the individual members of that community he is concerned through Jesus to produce people who are like Christ. Romans 8:29 states:

> For those God foreknew he also predestined to be conformed to the likeness of his Son, that he might be the firstborn among many brothers.

The role of the Spirit in this work of transformation is expressed clearly in 2 Corinthians 3:17–18 which reads:

> Now the Lord is the Spirit, and where the Spirit of the Lord is, there is freedom. And we, who with unveiled faces all reflect the Lord's glory, are being transformed into his likeness with ever-increasing glory, which comes from the Lord, who is the Spirit.

It is the Spirit's work to do in us what he has already done in Christ, but it is through Christ that this work is to be done. Christ has opened up a new relationship with God and has fulfilled and completed humanity. He is the true human being. The Spirit's work is to take what has been done in Jesus and reproduce it in those who believe, by making us conform to Christ's image. We shall see therefore that in describing the Spirit's work in the believer, there are some direct parallels with our description in Unit 4 of the Spirit's work in Christ.

THE SPIRIT'S PREPARATORY WORK

As the Spirit prepared the way for the coming of Christ into the world, so he prepares the way for us to come to the Father through Christ.

CONVICTING OF NEED

The Spirit of fellowship is about the task of restoring our broken relationship with the Father and to do this it is necessary to make us aware that we are lost and need to be reconciled to God. Jesus indicated that when the Spirit would come:

> He will convict the world of guilt in regard to sin and righteousness and judgment: in regard to sin, because men do not believe in me; in regard to righteousness because I am going to the Father, where you can see me no longer; and in regard to judgment, because the prince of this world now stands condemned (John 16:8–11).

Paraphrased, this means that the Spirit will show that people are sinners because of their unbelief in Christ, that Jesus is righteous and has been exalted, and that the ruler of this world has been judged at the cross. The Spirit's work is to convince people of the truth of these things and bring them to awareness of their need. This is what we see happening at Pentecost:

> When the people heard this, they were cut to the heart and said . . . 'Brothers, what shall we do?' (Acts 2:37).

Likewise, Paul says of the Thessalonians:

> . . . our gospel came to you not simply with words, but also with power, with the Holy Spirit and with deep conviction (1 Thess. 1:5).

Acts 2:37. Brothers, what shall we do?

TO THINK ABOUT . . .

It appears to many thoughtful Christians today that there is no widespread conviction of need or a sense of sin. Does this mean the Spirit is not at work? What other explanations could there be?

ENLIGHTENING MINDS

It is impossible for anyone to come to Christ unless the Father draws him (John 6:44). The Spirit of God is at work in the world drawing people to Christ, enlightening them (Eph. 1:17–18) and opening minds to the truth which is in Jesus (1 Cor. 2:8–10, 14–16). He is at work in us preparing the way for the Son of God to come and make his home within us.

TO THINK ABOUT . . .

Can you call to mind particular people, maybe for whom you have prayed, who show evidence that the Spirit of God is at work preparing them for faith?

THE SPIRIT'S REGENERATING WORK

The preparatory work of the Spirit has as its goal the regeneration, or new birth, of the individual. This is referred to in John 3:3–8 where Jesus teaches that a person can neither see nor enter the Kingdom of God unless born of the Spirit. The physical birth of individuals, bringing them into normal human life, must be paralleled by a spiritual birth which is not humanly produced but is the work of the Spirit. This work brings a person under the saving rule of God. It is accompanied by trust in Jesus Christ which opens the door into eternal life (John 3:16).

TO THINK ABOUT . . .

The paragraph above uses several terms which *you* may understand but which a non-Christian would find very strange – regeneration; new birth; Kingdom of God; born of the Spirit; saving rule of God; trust in Jesus Christ; eternal life.

How would you explain the ideas behind these terms in language which a non-Christian could understand?

THE MYSTERY OF HOW IT HAPPENS

When someone is born from above or of the Spirit there is a sense of mystery, just as there is when a baby is born. To think that in nine months a child can be conceived and develop into an amazingly complex individual is astonishing. So it is with new birth. There is a sense of mystery and wonder about the way a person becomes aware of needing God and then turns to him. We cannot fully explain it. We do not know why this person should come into new life in this way and at this time. This sense of wonder and of the sovereign freedom of God is what Jesus means when he refers to the Spirit as the wind:

> The wind blows wherever it pleases. You hear its sound, but you cannot tell where it comes from or where it is going. So it is with everyone who is born of the Spirit (John 3:8).

The result of this activity is that lives are inwardly changed. The new birth (or 'regeneration') is an inward change brought about by God in the hidden depths of the human personality. In another place it is described in this way:

> He saved us through the washing of rebirth and renewal of the Holy Spirit, whom he poured out on us generously through Jesus Christ our Saviour (Titus 3:5–6).

THE WORD BY WHICH IT HAPPENS

How all this comes to pass is a mystery to us, but it is clear that the Holy Spirit operates through the speaking of the gospel. So in Galatians 3:2 Paul says:

> Did you receive the Spirit by observing the law or by believing what you heard?

This is implied everywhere in the Bible but in Ephesians 6:17 it is clearly expressed:

> Take the helmet of salvation and the sword of the Spirit, which is the word of God.

True and accurate speaking of the gospel is the sharp edge by which the Spirit penetrates into people's lives. The close connection of Word and Spirit should not surprise us. We have seen that words need breath (spirit) in order to be uttered, that the creative Word was spoken into creation by the Spirit in the beginning and that the human life of Jesus, the Word of God, came to utterance, as it were, through the Spirit.

So it continues to be. The spoken word of the gospel receives its power and force through the Holy Spirit who is active in bringing people to new birth.

TO THINK ABOUT . . .

How limited is the Holy Spirit in his work by any inability of Christians to communicate the gospel in words clearly, simply and relevantly?

THE SPIRIT'S ADOPTING WORK

When a baby is born, he or she is the child of the parents. When believers are born of the Spirit, they become children of God. This means more than that they are forgiven. It is possible to be forgiven by someone and still not be a member of their family. But the love of God is such that when we receive his forgiveness he also makes us members of his family. It is the Holy Spirit who adopts us into God's family and brings us into personal union with the Father.

Romans 8:15 makes this clear:

> For you did not receive a spirit that makes you a slave again to fear, but you received the Spirit of sonship. And by him we cry 'Abba, Father'.

In Galatians 4:6 similar words occur:

> Because you are sons, God sent the Spirit of his son into our hearts, the Spirit who calls out, 'Abba, Father'.

ADOPTED INTO A NEW RELATIONSHIP

These verses from scripture are of the greatest importance. They show to us once more the intimate connection between the work of the Son and that of the Spirit. The Spirit is not at work independently of the Son but is drawing us through the Son into the relationship which the Son shares with the Father. What the believer receives through the Spirit is nothing less than living participation in the relationship between the Son and the Spirit.

This is made possible through the atoning life, death and resurrection of the Son. He came down and shared our fate so that through him we might be lifted into his relationship to the Father. What is made possible through the Son is made actual by the Spirit who relates us to the Father through the Son. We become God's children, sharing with the Son a living relationship to the Father, an access to his presence that heals and restores our broken lives.

> But now in Christ Jesus you who once were far away have been brought near through the blood of Christ . . . For through him we both (ie Jews and Gentiles) have access to the Father by one Spirit (Eph. 2:13, 18).

TO THINK ABOUT . . .

Is experiencing the Christian life as a relationship with God (Father, Son and Holy Spirit) more important than merely subscribing to a set of doctrinal statements about God?

Why do you answer in that way?

ADOPTED TO SHARE THE FELLOWSHIP OF GOD

Once more we see here the work of the Spirit of fellowship. The one who is the eternal bond of fellowship between Father and Son is the same who creates fellowship for human beings through the Son with the Father. 2 Peter 1:3–4 expresses it in this way:

> His divine power has given us everything we need for life and godliness through our knowledge of him who called us by his own glory and goodness. Through these he has given us his very great and precious promises, so that through them you may participate in the divine nature . . .

We participate in God as his children by the Spirit through the Son! A more amazing thought it is difficult to imagine.

THE SPIRIT'S ASSURING WORK

We are quickly led on to further thoughts. If God adopts us by his Spirit, it is that same Spirit who inwardly assures us that we are indeed children of God.

THE HEART STRANGELY WARMED

It would be presumptuous of us to claim this relationship were it not that the Spirit grants a deep, inward conviction that it is so. Not only does the Spirit create a spontaneous awareness that God is our 'Abba' or Father (Rom. 8:15); not only does he produce in us the spontaneous and intuitive recognition that we now know God in this way:

> The Spirit himself testifies with our spirit that we are God's children (Rom. 8:16).

These words speak of the Christian believer's experience of knowing profoundly and persuasively that he or she belongs to God. This is what John Wesley meant when he spoke of his heart being 'strangely warmed'. The experience defies explanation and must be understood as an awareness of the fellowship with God into which the Christian is brought through the Spirit.

TO THINK ABOUT . . .
The experience described here is more than just emotional 'feeling'. But how reliable or unreliable do you regard your feelings as a gauge of your spiritual state?

AN ANTIDOTE TO DOUBT

Every Christian will know the assuring work of the Spirit but all of us also know there are times when God seems more absent than present. To recognise that the Spirit is about the work of bringing assurance may help us to understand many experiences that are commonplace in the Church. Most of us need to experience some form of renewal at some time or other because our awareness of God wanes.

This explains why believers often testify to coming to a new place in their walk with God. Different terms have been used at different times. Sometimes people speak of being 'baptised in the Spirit', or 'sanctified'. Sometimes the renewal experience is accompanied by receiving a spiritual gift, such as speaking in tongues. It is helpful to see all these experiences as moments when the assurance of the Holy Spirit that we are truly in Christ and truly God's children is intensified and increased within us.

TO THINK ABOUT . . .
What moments or experiences can you recall in your Christian life when the Spirit has brought you deep assurance that you are truly in Christ and God's child?

What is the difference between assurance and self-confidence?

THE ASSURANCE JESUS KNEW

It is also humbling to note that Jesus himself knew moments of deep assurance. As a man 'tempted in every way, just as we are' (Heb. 4:15), he knew times of doubt and needed the assurance of the Spirit. It is possible to see the baptism of Jesus in this light:

> At that moment heaven was opened, and he saw the Spirit of God descending like a dove and lighting on him, And a voice from heaven said, 'This is my Son, whom I love; with him I am well pleased' (Matt. 3:16–17).

Similarly Luke 10:21–22 states:

> At that time, Jesus, full of joy through the Holy Spirit, said, I praise you, Father, Lord of heaven and earth . . . No-one knows who the Son is except the Father, and no-one knows who the Father is except the Son and those to whom the Son chooses to reveal him.

The assurance of his relationship with the Father which was impressed upon him by the Spirit is the same assurance into which every believer enters.

THE SPIRIT'S SANCTIFYING WORK

It is sometimes said that the crisis of the new birth needs to be followed by the process of being made holy. This is what is meant by sanctification. A person's life is radically changed from within to enable him or her to break with old, sinful patterns of living and to live a new, holy life in the power of God. The Spirit who initiated the new life is the one who sustains it. He is the *Holy* Spirit, the Spirit of holiness (Rom. 1:4).

DEFYING THE DOWNWARD DRAG

It is the Spirit who restrains the unholy tendencies with which we all struggle, keeping them in check by means of our willing co-operation:

> . . . Through Christ Jesus the law of the Spirit of life set me free from the law of sin and death . . . Those who live according to the sinful nature have

their minds set on what that nature desires; but those who live in accordance with the Spirit have their minds set on what the Spirit desires. The mind of sinful man is death, but the mind controlled by the Spirit is life and peace . . . You, however, are controlled not by the sinful nature but by the Spirit, if the Spirit of God lives in you, And if anyone does not have the Spirit of Christ, he does not belong to Christ (Rom. 8:2, 5–6, 9).

The Spirit, who is present in the life of every believing person, is the active and powerful influence of God holding at bay our sinful tendencies. We may think of this as the principle of flight which enables an aeroplane to rise above the law of gravity. In the same way, by the Spirit, the downward drag of our sinful tendencies is overcome as we live in the power of the Spirit of God, the 'law of the Spirit of life' which sets us free from the 'law of sin and death'.

TO THINK ABOUT . . .

To what extent is the Spirit's ministry to get us 'airborne' as it were *helped* by our willing co-operation or *hindered* by our lack of it?

Think of specific examples.

POWER FOR THE GOOD LIFE

The Spirit not only restrains the evil that is in us, he releases into us the power to do that which is good:

> So, I say, live by the Spirit, and you will not gratify the desires of the sinful nature . . . the fruit of the Spirit is love, joy, peace, patience, kindness, goodness, faithfulness, gentleness and self-control (Gal. 5:16, 22–23).

The term 'fruit of the Spirit' helps us to see that the virtues listed are the result, or the harvest, of the Spirit's presence in our lives. He causes them to spring forth from within us. If we wished to summarise these virtues we could simply say that they amount to being like Christ, in whom we see these qualities held together in perfect harmony. The Spirit renews us into the image of Jesus Christ so that we are progressively changed into his likeness (2 Cor. 3:18).

TO THINK ABOUT . . .
'The fruits of the Spirit are the virtues of Christ'. From what you know of the life of Christ in the Gospels, what would you pick out as the main features of his character?

THE FRUIT OF THE SPIRIT

We might conveniently divide the fruit of the Spirit into inner and outer qualities.

Inner Qualities

Some of those which Paul lists are part of the inner experience of the believer, particularly the qualities of joy and peace. The Spirit creates a disposition within the Christian which replaces the common experiences of dejection and unrest with the joy and peace which come from knowing that through peace with God all is well. It would also be true to say that no Christian experiences these emotions all the time, nor should they. But all Christians will find themselves occasionally being surprised by deep feelings of joy or of peace, and most have a sense of underlying security in God, despite the outer circumstances. All this comes from the Spirit who upholds and undergirds our lives.

Outer Qualities

The inner dispositions find outward expression in the other qualities Paul mentions of which the first listed is of course love, that attitude which actively seeks the good of others. In a sense, the qualities which follow are simply commentaries on what the loving life looks like. The loving life is patient and kind towards others, desires and seeks only that which is good, is reliable and dependable and is not subject to unpredictable moods or likely to fly off the handle. This is what we see in Jesus and this is what the Spirit is doing in us. Indeed, such qualities are the only infallible signs of the presence of the Spirit.

TO THINK ABOUT . . .
In which area of life (home, work, community, school, church) do you find it hardest to be a consistent Christian? What makes it hard? Which aspects of the Fruit of the Spirit are most needed there?

Paul makes it abundantly clear that although the Christian may experience all manner of remarkable things, the only absolutely certain sign of the Spirit of God is the love which is reproduced by him in our lives. This is particularly the point in 1 Corinthians 13 where Paul is helping folk to see that, although God may well be at work in dramatic and miraculous events, everything which is dramatic and marvellous is not necessarily of God. Rather we are to look for love as the sign of his true presence.

. . . let us not love with words or tongue but with actions and in truth (1 John 3:18).

It is also noteworthy that in Galalatians 5:22 Paul refers to the 'fruit' (singular) of the Spirit not the 'fruits' (plural). In other words, the virtues which he lists are not various options, one or other of which may be found in the Spirit-controlled life. They are the fruit of the Spirit all of which qualities are found together in harmony and unity in the life which is truly given over to God.

Inevitably when we read this we end up asking what is wrong with us. None of us matches up to the description Paul gives. But if the Spirit is within us, all of us are on the road towards being made completely like Christ.

This capacity to be and do good is one which is not humanly generated. It is a gift from God. It comes about when we live in dependence on the Spirit of God. Just as he is the breath of God that upholds creation and enables it to be, so he is the Spirit who upholds Christians and enables them to live in and for God.

ENABLING SACRIFICIAL LIVING

This way of living is a million miles away from the form of legalism which sees the good life as a series of rules to be obeyed. It is living for God because something has happened which makes us want to do so. It is the fulfilment of the Old Testament prophecy:

> I will put my law in their minds and write it on their hearts. I will be their God and they will be my people (Jer. 31:33).

It is the Holy Spirit who writes God's holy will upon the hearts of those who believe and causes them to will that which is right. This includes enabling believers to live sacrificially. In considering the Spirit's work in Christ we noted that 'through the eternal Spirit (he) offered himself unblemished to God' (Heb. 9:14). The self-offering of Jesus was motivated by the Spirit and Christians likewise are enabled to give themselves to God and for others in sacrificial service because of the Spirit within them.

TO THINK ABOUT . . .

The picture above is of Frank Darling's grave in Matadi, Zaire. He died aged 29 whilst on pioneer missionary service in Africa.

The following is an extract from a letter written by a BMS missionary currently serving as a doctor at the Pimu Hospital in Zaire. He is discussing the point that in the days when missionaries died overseas there was no lack of candidates either!

> It might be today that with modern trends in worship we create a nice comfortable Christianity that keeps us going from week to week at home, but does not prepare us for hardship or sacrifice. Paul sang his worship songs in prison as well as with the congregations he founded.

> . . . if you come here you will be committing suicide in your career, you will be working hard for your own demotion and handing your job to someone less qualified than yourself, and you might even die.

A colleague in the Department of Tropical Medicine says statistically I should be HIV positive in the next ten years, if I continue doing surgery in Zaire. So I will not live to receive my BMS pension! I thought he was joking until I tried topping up that pension with a little life assurance and the Company would not even give me a ten year policy if I stayed in Zaire.

> . . . will anyone put their faith into commitment and their commitment into sacrifice and come and help us?

What impact do the extracts above make on your life? How do you respond to the statement that modern trends in worship do not prepare God's people for hardship or sacrifice?

THE SPIRIT'S EMPOWERING WORK

The Holy Spirit is forever associated with the powerful events of the Day of Pentecost and with the words of Jesus:

> But you will receive power when the Holy Spirit comes on you; and you will be my witnesses in Jerusalem, and in all Judea and Samaria, and to the ends of the earth (Acts 1:8).

This promise of power for witness comes in intimate relation with the preceding words:

> For John baptised with water, but in a few days you will be baptised with the Holy Spirit (Acts 1:5).

The phrase 'baptise with the Holy Spirit' raises an issue which has figured large in recent debate. The charismatic movement has insisted on the need to be 'baptised with the Spirit', that is to have an empowering experience of the same order as that of the disciples at Pentecost. We have already examined this subject in a preliminary way. The issues are really quite complex, but it might help to set out three options for defining 'the baptism of the Spirit'.

TO THINK ABOUT . . .
Before continuing, think over how you understand the term 'baptism (with its associations with water) of the Spirit'.

EMPOWERING AND EQUIPPING

Charismatic Christians have often (but by no means always) argued that baptism in the Spirit is that part of the Spirit's work which has to do with empowering and equipping. Every Christian needs to be endued with power and this should be seen as a definite experience and not just something that all Christians theoretically possess. The danger has been that of dividing up Christians into two classes – those baptised in the Spirit and those not. Other Christians have rightly found this latter implication difficult to accept. Charismatics have tended to appeal to Acts to justify their position.

REGENERATION

The second option has been to insist that baptism in the Spirit is not an empowering work but regeneration. Every Christian is regenerated by the Spirit and baptised into Christ and therefore there cannot be two classes of Christians. Baptism in the Spirit is conversion.

Those who take this position appeal to Paul and particularly to 1 Corinthians 12:13 which announces:

> we were all baptised by one Spirit into one body.

To insist that people need to be baptised in the Spirit, when they already are, seems disrespectful to them. It seems almost like saying that someone who is a Christian needs to become a Christian.

This position makes it clear that all Christians belong to the same class, but it obscures the fact that they do need to be empowered. The Christian does not become complete at conversion. To say: 'there is nothing else I need' is a perilously dangerous spiritual position to take. To safeguard against this, some prefer to speak of 'being filled with the Spirit' as does Paul in Ephesians 5:18. All Christians may be baptised in the Spirit, but not all are filled with the Spirit. The problem then is that the promise of Jesus in Acts 1:5–9 (which we see fulfilled in Acts 2:1ff) seems to indicate that baptism in the Spirit is a very powerful event.

The fact of the matter is that if all Christians have been baptised with the Spirit, many of them appear not to have noticed!

A FLUID INTERPRETATION

A third option recognises that in the New Testament the idea of the baptism of the Spirit is fuller than we realise. It is a fluid term which points to the life-changing reality of life in the Spirit of God.

Sometimes it is used with overtones of regeneration (1 Cor. 12:13). On other occasions it has overtones of spiritual empowering (Acts 1:5, 8). Basically it is a metaphor for the reality of new life and new power into which we are plunged when we are converted. It is an inclusive term which refers to the totality of spiritual reality which the Spirit begins in us.

So it is difficult to use the term of only one part of the Spirit's work. Water baptism speaks about the work of the Spirit. As we are plunged into the water, so we are plunged by Christ into the realm of the Spirit. It can be argued, therefore, that all Christians have been baptised in the Spirit (*ie.* have entered into new life) and also that all Christians need to be baptised in the Spirit (*ie.* to enter into the experience of the Spirit's power). This may sound like saying everybody is right. Actually it is saying that the truth about the Spirit is bigger than all of us. Those who disagree over this subject may well be stressing different aspects of the total truth.

> ### TO THINK ABOUT . . .
> Does this fluid interpretation of 'the baptism of the Spirit' satisfy you? How true is the last sentence of the paragraph above? If it is true, how should it affect your attitude to those with whom you disagree?

THE SPIRIT'S 'COMING'

Part of the problem of understanding the Spirit's work comes because we are too wooden in the way we think. The Spirit of God is living, dynamic, moving. He is the Spirit who is sent out into the world to draw us through the Son to the Father. To enter into his life is to enter into this dynamic movement, to be caught up by him into God.

We need to be cautious about defining the Spirit too closely. Jesus reminded us that he is like the wind and cannot be taken hold of (John 3:8). We may describe his work but cannot define it. Whatever opinion we have, if we say 'this is how the Spirit works and if it isn't like this it can't be the Spirit', then we are trying to imprison the wind.

The folly of trying to catch the wind.

> ### TO THINK ABOUT . . .
> How comfortable are you with the caution against defining the Spirit too closely? What are the dangers in claiming that we can describe his work but cannot define it?

An alternative model for understanding might be to change the language and speak of the Spirit's 'coming'. The Spirit comes to people when they are first converted: this may be called his 'definitive' coming. But we need the Spirit to keep on coming to us and therefore need to be open to his new comings.

Moreover, the comings of the Spirit may vary in intensity and from occasion to occasion. Christians are those to whom the Spirit of God has come, yet they are those to whom the dynamic Spirit of God goes on coming to renew, intensify, deepen and increase that which was given in his first coming. There is plenty of room for the work of the Spirit after conversion, and no Christian should doubt that there is always more of God in Christ into which the Spirit wants to bring us.

THE SPIRIT'S EQUIPPING WORK

When the Spirit of God comes he brings gifts to enable us to serve. We have already examined this subject in some measure but some further comment is appropriate:

> Now to each one the manifestation of the Spirit is given for the common good (1 Cor. 12:7).

RESPONSIBILITY FOR IMPARTING GIFTS – HIS

In 1 Corinthians 12 Paul emphasises the free, dynamic and spontaneous way in which the Spirit imparts whatever he wills, to whomever he wills, whenever he wills (vv.7–11). His point is that whatever the Spirit imparts is gift. No-one has reason to boast or imagine him- or herself superior to others, since we have nothing that we did not receive.

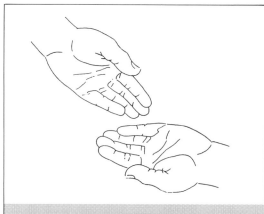

TO THINK ABOUT . . .
Think of ways in which your hands, by serving, helping and giving, can be instruments of the Holy Spirit's ministry.

TO THINK ABOUT . . .
Look at 1 Cor. 12:14–20. How does Paul's teaching guard against the peril not only of superiority but also of inferiority in relation to the Spirit's gifts?

The gifts which the Spirit brings, many and diverse as they are, are given so that the presence of Jesus Christ may be known as a reality within his body. It is unhelpful to imagine that such gifts are solely vocal in nature. They include serving, helping and giving (Rom. 12:7–8). They are the many and concrete ways in which Christ by his Spirit draws near through the people who are his. Spiritual gifts can therefore only be rightly employed in love (1 Cor. 13).

RESPONSIBILITY FOR USING GIFTS – OURS

Although *of* the Spirit, the Spirit's action does not deprive individuals of responsible involvement in the manifestation of spiritual gifts. We cannot claim that 'the Spirit made me do it' since:

> the spirits of prophets are subject to the control of prophets (1 Cor. 14:32).

This means that, although there may be times when the Spirit powerfully constrains us, we cannot blame irresponsible actions on him. God is a God of peace and not of disorder and we remain responsible for the ways in which we respond to the workings of the Spirit in us (1 Cor. 14:26–33).

TO THINK ABOUT . . .
Why is it that Paul has to write 1 Corinthians 13 between chapters 12 and 14? What is it about spiritual gifts that requires this emphasis on love?

THE SPIRIT'S INTERCEDING WORK

Significant in this respect are Paul's word in Romans 8:26–27:

> In the same way the Spirit helps us in our weakness. We do not know what we ought to pray for, but the Spirit himself intecedes for us with groans that words cannot express. And he who searches our hearts knows the mind of the Spirit, because the Spirit intercedes for the saints in accordance with God's will.

Later in the chapter he tells us that the Son of God prays for us (8:34). Here he tells us that the Spirit of God, the divine current of communication between the Father and the Son, prays in us. When we know neither what to pray nor how to pray, the Spirit knows the will of God and in ways deeper than words interprets our inner longings to the Father.

The Spirit therefore is intimately involved with the activity of prayer and supports and undergirds us in our praying. Whereas we are inclined to think of prayer as a chore or a duty which must be performed, these words teach us that prayer is a gracious gift from God. When we are conscious of the inadequacy of our prayers, these words speak of the help of the Spirit in making them adequate.

We should think of prayer as a conversation taking place within God in which we are enabled to participate and to which we contribute by the Spirit of God. This is the conversation which we see taking place in Luke 10:21 and to which Jesus indicates, in 10:22–24, we also will gain access.

> **TO THINK ABOUT . . .**
> **How could these ideas encourage and strengthen your prayer life?**

THE SPIRIT'S RESURRECTING WORK

The final aspect of the Spirit's work which we outline concerns a future work we have yet to see. As the Spirit was the means whereby Jesus was raised out of death (1 Pet. 3:18), so he is the one through whom believers will be restored to full personal existence in a glorified form. We call this the resurrection:

> And if the Spirit of him who raised Jesus from the dead is living in you, he who raised Christ from the dead will also give life to your mortal bodies through his Spirit, who lives in you (Rom. 8:11).

How all this is to be passes our understanding. What it is like to live in a spiritual body (1 Cor. 15:44), we do not know.

We can, however, gain some clues from the resurrection of Jesus whose physical body was both transformed and glorified, while remaining recognisably that which he possessed in his earthly life. Possibly his body was still undergoing transformation during the resurrection appearances. It is fair to conclude that a similar transformation of believers will be accomplished by the Spirit who will complete the work of which 1 Corinthians 15:49 speaks:

> And just as we have borne the likeness of the earthly man, so shall we bear the likeness of the man from heaven.

> **TO THINK ABOUT . . .**
> **How do you feel about your body:**
>
> > **full of wonder?**
> > **proud?**
> > **embarrassed?**
> > **frustrated?**
> > **angry?**
> > **grateful?**
> > **some other response?**
>
> **What features would you like the resurrection body to have and why?**

With this tentative examination of the resurrection we draw to a close our survey of the Spirit's work in the individual. In doing so we stress once more the practical value of what we have considered. If the Spirit is so completely and intimately involved in fulfilling God's saving purposes in us, the only way we can live is in absolute dependence on God the Spirit for life, holiness, power, gifts, guidance and the future.

ASSIGNMENT 4

Discerning the Work of the Spirit of God in Today's World

Jonathan Edwards reasoned that any movement was of God if it showed the following characteristics:

- a desire to honour Jesus Christ;
- opposition to sin, the world and the power of evil;
- reverence for the Bible as the Word of God;
- emphasis on the urgency of eternal issues;
- new love for Christ and for others.

In this assignment you are asked to construct your own criteria for recognising the Spirit at work (use any of Edwards' characteristics if you wish) and then use your criteria to indicate how you see the Spirit at work in the modern world in any *one* of the following areas:

1. the world of art, literature and music (or you may choose any one of these);
2. contemporary concern for ecological issues;
3. movement towards political and social liberation;
4. present day trends in the church.

Your completed work should be about 1000 words in length.

UNIT 8

The Spirit and the Future

THE FINAL ASPECT of our study is possibly the most difficult, since it concerns that which is yet to be. We have prepared for this by considering the Spirit's work in resurrection. The Spirit is the one through whom we will be raised from death. We can hardly imagine how this will be, although the fact that Jesus has already been raised helps us.

In this unit we go on to make the claim that the future belongs to the Spirit. It is significant that in the creed, faith in the Holy Spirit as the life-giver is confessed in the same section as the life everlasting. The Spirit is the forward thrust who draws the whole of creation to its ultimate goal of unification in Christ and submission to the Father (Eph. 1:10; 1 Cor. 15:28).

> **TO THINK ABOUT . . .**
> What does the statement 'the future belongs to the Spirit' mean? In what ways is the Spirit the 'down-payment' of what is to come (Ephesians 1:13–14)?

THE SPIRIT'S FORWARD THRUST

This may be understood as follows: It is biblical and traditional to think of the Spirit as coming into the world from the Father through the Son (Father > Son > Spirit). With the Spirit, however, we find a pivot on which the whole of the world turns. After Pentecost the Spirit furthers the work of salvation by restoring all things through Christ to the Father (Spirit > Son > Father). The Spirit comes to us through the Son in order that through the Son he might restore the world to the Father. This work will only be accomplished in the fullness of time and is looked forward to as:

the time . . . for God to restore everything as he promised long ago through his holy prophets (Acts 3:21).

PROPHETIC VISION

The prophets speak of this time in many differing ways. It is the time when the lion and the lamb will lie down together and none will hurt or destroy, when:

the earth will be full of the knowledge of the Lord as the waters cover the sea (Isaiah 11:6–9).

> **TO THINK ABOUT . . .**
> The lion lying down with the lamb is one way of expressing the restored order of the future.
>
> What images and pictures help you to anticipate and visualise that time?

It will be the age when life-giving water will flow into all the world, bringing fruitfulness and healing (Ezekiel 47); when darkness will be abolished and the Lord's name will be the only name (Zechariah 14:6–9); when the earth will be filled with the glory of the Lord (Habakkuk 2:14). With many glorious images the prophets point us forward to a time when conflict and fear will be abolished and the world will be transformed into an ultimate harmony in Father, Son and Holy Spirit. This time is the new heaven and new earth in which righteousness dwell (Isaiah 65:17; 2 Peter 3:13).

TO THINK ABOUT . . .

How should the future affect the present? In what ways is the present shaped for the Christian not only by past events but also by the Bible's teaching about the future?

That it is the Spirit's particular work to draw all things towards this ultimate goal may be generally understood from all that we have previously said about the Spirit. As the Spirit at work in creating the world and in recreating the Church in the image of Christ, he is the active presence of God bringing God's purposes to pass. Specifically, the Spirit is related to this future age in Joel 2:28–32. The pouring out of the Spirit on all flesh is here linked to 'the coming great and dreadful day of the LORD' (v.31) with its attendant upheavals in the created sphere.

PRESENT FORETASTE

Joel's prophecy is seen by Peter to be in process of fulfilment on the day of Pentecost (Acts 2: 16–21). The point he makes is that the Spirit who is associated with the final day of the Lord has actually come in the here and now to bring salvation. This corresponds to Paul's teaching about the Spirit as a down-payment of what is to come:

> He anointed us, set his seal of ownership on us, and put his Spirit in our hearts as a deposit, guaranteeing what is to come (2 Cor. 1:21–22; see also 5:5).

Similarly:

> Having believed, you were marked in him with a seal, the promised Holy Spirit, who is a deposit guaranteeing our inheritance until the redemption of those who are God's possession – to the praise of his glory (Eph. 1:13–14).

The knowledge of the Spirit now is a foretaste of the final unification of all things by the Spirit in the Son with the Father.

THE SPIRIT AS 'TRANSCREATOR'

One way of expressing this aspect of the Spirit's work is to see the Spirit as the 'Transcreator'. Because the Spirit is involved in creation it is right to see him as Creator-Spirit. Because he renews us in the image of Christ it is also right to see him as the Recreator-Spirit. He is also the Transcreator in that through him the world is being transformed towards its ultimate goal in Christ. The Spirit is the one who is crossing the gaps and who will one day close the gap of alienation in the world to restore all things to the Father.

Of course all this needs to be seen in intimate connection with the Father and the Son as they work together for the fulfilment of the divine purpose. We have already noted that the Spirit is the Spirit of fellowship and in this transcreative work we see him making for the fellowship of all things with the Father through the Son. This is the ultimate salvation for which we hope and of which we have the 'deposit'.

We shall conclude this discussion by showing the perspectives to which it leads us.

A PERSPECTIVE ON OURSELVES

Because we are those who have received the Spirit, we are those who have entered in the here and now into the peace which will one day be shared by the whole creation (Rom. 5:1–5). The Holy Spirit has been poured into our hearts bringing confident hope that one day all creation will be at peace.

A PERSPECTIVE ON THE CHURCH

The Church is that community of the Spirit which is in the world now as a sign of the ultimate reconciliation of all things (Eph. 2:14–22). The Spirit is already making us into the kind of community that will inherit the earth. The Church lives in the Spirit. It anticipates the reunion of all humanity in Christ (Matt. 8:11). It shares together in the feast of bread and wine which is a foretaste of the recreation of the heavens and the earth (Matt. 26:29; Rev. 19:9, 17). It lives not according to the pattern of the alienated world in this age but in love and justice according to the power of the age that will be (Rom. 12:1–2).

> **TO THINK ABOUT . . .**
> Call to mind ways in which your church is a sign and foretaste of what God plans for his world.
>
> Are you:
>
> > encouraged?
> > disappointed?
> > challenged?
> > grateful?
> > despairing?
> > some other response?

A PERSPECTIVE ON THE WORLD

As the world has its being in the Spirit we are entitled to see him at work beyond the confines of the church in every act of humanity, every movement towards a more just, Christlike existence, everything that is good and fine, gathering all things together and drawing them forward to the restoration of all things. While he is at work first and foremost and explicitly in the Church, he is also at work implicitly in everything that harmonises with Christ in the world at large.

This is one of the bases on which Christians should involve themselves in all that makes for justice and peace, believing that in doing so they are working together with God the Spirit towards the day of final redemption. To have this perspective is a constant reminder that the Lord who is the Spirit is present throughout his creation.

> **TO THINK ABOUT . . .**
> To think in this way is to do so in very broad terms of the Spirit's work. Is this warranted? If so, can you see the Spirit at work at all in the political events of the present?

In Revelation 22 we are given a glorious vision of the end of all things and of God's final victory. We read:

> Then the angel showed me the river of the water of life, as clear as crystal, flowing from the throne of God and of the Lamb down the middle of the great street of the city. On each side of the river stood the tree of life bearing twelve crops of fruit yielding its fruit each month. And the leaves of the tree are for the healing of the nations (vv.1–2).

In this vision the crystal river represents the Spirit. Wherever the river flows it brings life, healing and abundance. The warrings of the nations and their ancient scars are healed because of the life-giving water. So it is with the Spirit who flows to us from Father and Son to bring all things to their ultimate and glorious goal in the knowledge of God. So not only the prophecies of Scripture but the longings of our hearts and of the whole creation find their fulfilment in the eternal presence of the everliving God, Father, Son and Spirit.

> **TO THINK ABOUT . . .**
> Reflect again on the words 'In him we live and move and have our being'. The world has its being for God and in him by the Spirit. How will this affect your life in the future?

CONCLUSION

We began this study with the intention of testing against Scripture the Church's existing conclusion that the Holy Spirit is both truly personal and truly God. The evidence we have examined bears this out. According to Christian faith, therefore, the Holy Spirit is to be honoured and adored in union with the Father and the Son as God. In the words of the Nicene Creed: 'I believe in the Holy Spirit . . . who with the Father and the Son together is to be worshipped and glorified.'

To honour the Holy Spirit is not purely a matter of theology. Where he is most honoured, he is most free to fulfil his mission of glorifying Jesus Christ in the lives of those who believe, drawing them to the Father through him. It is not simply correct but of vital importance to the well-being of the Church that the Spirit receive his rightful place in our thinking, our worship and our lives. The words of the hymn are appropriate:

> **All praise to God the Father be,**
> **All praise eternal Son to Thee,**
> **Whom with the Spirit we adore,**
> **For ever and for evermore. Amen.**

FURTHER READING

Comblin, Jose, *The Holy Spirit and Liberation* (Tunbridge Wells, 1989)

Dunn, James, *Jesus and the Spirit: A Study of the Religious and Charismatic Experience of Jesus and the First Christians as Reflected in the New Testament* (London, 1975)

Fiddes, Paul, *Charismatic Renewal: A Baptist View* (London, 1980)

Green, Michael, *I Believe in the Holy Spirit* (London, 1975)

Heron, Alasdair, *The Holy Spirit: The Holy Spirit in the Bible, in the History of Christian Thought and in recent Theology* (London, 1983)

Moltmann, Jurgen, *The Church in the Power of the Holy Spirit* (London, 1977)

Packer, James, *Keep in Step with the Spirit* (Leicester, 1984)

——, Article 'Piety on Fire' *Renewal* July 1990 pp.28–32

Rosato, Philip J., *The Spirit as Lord: The Pneumatology of Karl Barth* (Edinburgh, 1981)

——, Article 'The Holy Spirit' in *A New Dictionary of Christian Theology* edited by Alan Richardson and John Bowden (London, 1983)

Smail, Thomas, *Reflected Glory: The Spirit in Christ and Christians* (London, 1975)

——, *The Giving Gift: The Holy Spirit in Person* (London, 1988)

Taylor, John, *The Go-Between God: The Holy Spirit and the Christian Mission* (London, 1972)